Financial
WISDOM

9 Timeless Principles of Personal
and Business Finances

TIM POLLOCK

WestBow
PRESS
A DIVISION OF THOMAS NELSON

WestBow Press books may be ordered through booksellers or by contacting:

WestBow Press
A Division of Thomas Nelson
1663 Liberty Drive
Bloomington, IN 47403
www.westbowpress.com
1-(866) 928-1240

ISBN: 978-1-4908-0227-5 (sc)
ISBN: 978-1-4908-0228-2 (e)

Library of Congress Control Number: 2013912978

Printed in the United States of America.

WestBow Press rev. date: 8/29/2013

TABLE OF CONTENTS

DEDICATION

To my amazing family and wife, Lynette (who is now with the Lord), Pauline, and church. Without your love and support, I would fail. I love you and thank God for you!

PREFACE

This book, *Financial Wisdom*, is my heart. For some strange reason, I continuously feel a special calling from the Lord to a life of extreme faith in the area of family and ministry. Almost thirty years ago, I was reading in Luke 16 about being faithful with mammon so God can trust us with true riches. I purposed as I contemplated those words that day to know everything I could about finances from the Book of books! As you work prayerfully through the pages of *Financial Wisdom*, you will gain insight into my spiritual journey. I think I have made every mistake possible financially, relationally, and in ministry. While I have had many failures, I also know by God's grace how to achieve victory.

The Lord has blessed me with a wonderful, large family (twelve children, thirty grandchildren, and counting)! Between our family and the multiplied thousands of people through the years I have preached to, talked to, and counseled, I have learned some great lessons. My voyage is not one of one unbroken success but a chronicle of God's faithfulness through the good and the bad days.

While I have enjoyed so many of life's blessings, I have also been tested by the fires of deep adversity. After a four-year pilgrimage of ups and downs, I watched my childhood sweetheart and wife of thirty-four years slip into the arms of Jesus as she died of breast cancer at the age of fifty-four. This tragedy, however, turned into triumph. Through the dark night of heartache, God rebirthed in me a desire to think and act biblically as well as reach out to those who are hurting relationally and financially. To God be all the glory, He brought into my life a wonderful Christian lady, who had lost her husband, and we are moving ahead hand in hand to make a difference our remaining years on earth.

Pastors and laypeople have asked me many questions about how we built a large campus of buildings debt free with volunteer labor. Many people have also wondered how we could make a large family work on a modest single income. All I can say is that God's Word works if you work it! My prayer is that you will be so blessed by this journey of the nine most important financial principles from the Bible.

INTRODUCTION

PERSONAL FINANCE IS A very real part of our lives. Money is wrapped into everything we do. It is something we think about several times a day, or more. There is much about the use of our money that affects us physically, emotionally, and relationally.

In the early part of my life, I remember being very concerned about the morals of money. I knew that when our morals aren't right, nothing goes well, because the fear of the Lord is the *beginning* of wisdom (Proverbs 9:10) KJV. But what I also have discovered is that God's Word is integrative. Our moral principles and our day-to-day lives actually run on parallel tracks. What I mean by that is our bodies, souls, and spirits are almost inseparable. What goes on in our heads, hearts, and spirits also affect our bodies. Therefore, it also touches our finances.

I'm so glad God in His Word has given us the answers about everything we will face in this life, including our finances. God has given specific, practical principles for every era that always work. You might be surprised to learn there are over fifteen hundred verses concerning money (or its equivalent) in the Bible! One day I started searching for everything the Bible says about having good financial health. I discovered some amazing things. For example, did you know Jesus talked about finances more than any other single subject? This means there is more Scripture dedicated to money principles than about heaven, hell, or the Trinity. Money is so much a part of who we are. Someone once said, "Don't tell me how you live. Let me see your checkbook, and I'll tell you how you live." How we spend our money is the single most accurate biography of our lives.

Financial Wisdom is a collection of money principles from the book of Proverbs. Solomon (the human author) is known in biblical history as the wisest man who ever lived. This book was likely written in the latter years of Solomon's life. God used the personal experiences from Solomon's life in the area of business, faith, family, finances, and more.

As we begin this discussion, a basic, guiding parameter is needed in order to start making winning financial choices. The number-one question we must ask ourselves is, "Is it wise? Is it biblical?" Sometimes we wrongly surmise God's Word is really good when it comes to morals, but if you really want to know how to win financially, you need to go to a secular financial counselor. Financial counselors can give some good advice at times that works. The wonderful thing about God's principles, however, are that they work all the time!

A story has been told of an angel who appeared at a faculty meeting and told a dean that, in return for his unselfish service, he would be rewarded with the choice of wealth, wisdom, or beauty. Without hesitating, the dean chose wisdom, "It is done," the angel said. In a cloud of smoke, the angel disappeared. One of the faculty members ventured out and whispered, "Dean, now that you have infinite wisdom, say something." The dean looked at each of them and said, "I should have taken the money!" You, too, may appreciate Bible wisdom but think what you really need is money. I believe God has some great wisdom for us that is practical and profitable at the same time.

The greatest protection and benefit for our financial well-being is to purpose in our hearts that we will *always* do what God says. In the book of Proverbs alone, there is over 150 verses on money, divided into nine categories. Let's begin prayerfully and obediently.

CHAPTER 1

Financial Wisdom Principle #1
Watch Out for Destructive Influences

WE CHRISTIANS ARE OFTEN gullible. I hate to say that, but it's true. Too often we allow our mercy to override our prudence. We lose the common sense of doing things wisely. I like the preacher who said, "I may be born again, but I wasn't born yesterday!" There's nothing wrong with having worldly smarts along with the Bible's wonderful, practical wisdom.

1. Exercise Caution with Friends

> We shall find all precious substance, we shall fill
> our house with spoil. (Proverbs 1:13)

It's important to note that the very first financial principle God gives in Proverbs is to be cautious. There are a lot of destructive influences in the world today. Notice the word *we*. It's been well said that when a person with experience and one with money get together, the individual with experience gets the money, and the one with the money gets a new experience! Next, see the word *shall*. *Shall* is a guarantee. In this particular verse, the word *shall* is a guarantee of financial prosperity. When someone starts saying words like *guaranteed investment* or *guaranteed cure*, we must take things slowly. You and I both know there is no such thing as a guaranteed investment or cure. These swindlers go on to refer to a "precious substance" that will be gotten. Well, it's not really precious compared to the wisdom of God. The things of this earth are certainly not of highest value. Interestingly enough, the substance is not even real. The things of the earth only last for a few hours, days, months, or years. But true value and eternal things last forever. When you really think about it, everything that person said was off base.

We all like stuff; we like to fill our houses with substance. If one couch is good, three are better; if one TV is good, five are better. The Devil is out to rob us of much-needed resources for higher-priority items. I have had some crazy experiences over the years with people trying to separate me from my money. I wish I could say I always saw it coming. When my wife had breast cancer, some well-meaning people, and a few others, guaranteed healing. Of course, all you have to do is Google "cancer cures" on the Internet, and you will get millions of results. Many people out there absolutely guarantee healing for cancer. If that were really the case, there would be no cancer. I'm not saying some alternative remedies can't be helpful; they can. In fact, most of the major medicines we use come from God-created substances. Aspirin, for example, comes from willow bark. However, medicine doesn't always work all the time for all people. And we must be careful, especially at such a vulnerable time, not to buy into all the hype.

Another area of destructive influence I have personally experienced is aggressive multilevel marketing. I know many wonderful, honest people who work from home in non-traditional ways but this person turned out to be not so ethical. When I was in my twenties, a man came to my office and asked with mock concern, "What are your dreams?" I naively thought how nice it was for this person to care about my future.

"Would you like to have some extra money for your family? Would you like freedom? Would you like to spend more time with your children?" he continued. My initial reaction was that, of course, I wanted these things. Who wouldn't? I have since learned, however, these extreme marketers are trained to appeal to the things you are likely feeling in your current circumstances. Without divulging any specifics, he stated, "Let me come over to your house and share a business opportunity with you." The opportunity, as he called it, turned out to be a business of signing up as many of my friends and family as possible to be business representatives who would, in turn, do the same. It was making merchandise of my relationships. No thanks!

The Massachusetts Lottery Company ran the following advertisement.

> Plan "A": start studying when you're about seven, study really hard. Grow up to get a good job, get up at dawn every day to flatter your boss, crush the competition ruthlessly, climb over the backs of co-workers, be the last one to leave every night, squirrel away every cent, avoid having a nervous breakdown or premature heart attack, get a face lift, do this every day for 30 years (holidays and weekends included), and by the time you're ready

to retire, maybe you'll have some money. Or, Plan "B": play the lottery.

Sadly, even the government at times joins other tricksters in acquiring our God-given resources.

2. Steer Clear of Seductive Relationships

> Strangers shall be filled with thy wealth, and thy labors shall be in the house of a stranger. (Proverbs 5:10)

One of the most painful types of financial problems results from impure relationships. Solomon would know. Scripture records that Solomon had seven hundred wives and three hundred concubines. In many cases, it is thought he married for money; that is, he entered into matrimony with the daughters of neighboring kings for political and financial gains. But instead of growing his resources, he discovered it was often exactly the opposite. Pleasure for a moment can turn into pain for a lifetime.

God made us to be stewards of His resources. He gave us the responsibility to protect our family. To give away hard-won resources because we've gotten involved in a marriage-breaking relationship is a huge, unnecessary loss. There are some who for years have had a messy financial life because they are still paying on the tragedy of loose morals. A good biblical example is found in Genesis 34. The covetous sons of Jacob developed a sinister plan of lust involving their sisters that not only destroyed their enemy but got their wealth, too.

We need the grace of God to steer clear of tempting relationships. God reminds us that one of the tragic results of letting down your moral walls is that your wealth will be in the house of a stranger (Proverbs 5:10).

Here's a story that will make you chuckle about relationships with the wrong person. An enraptured fellow wanted to get married—he had the ring in his hand—and he told his girlfriend, "Sweetheart, I love you so much. I want you to marry me! I don't have a car or a yacht like Johnny Green. I don't have a house that's near the size he has. I certainly don't have the amount of money he has, either, but I love you with all of my heart." She looked into his eyes and said, "I love you, too. Could you tell me a little bit more about Johnny Green?"

3. Be Careful, Little Tongue, What You Say

> My son, if thou be surety for a friend ...
> (Proverbs 6:1)

The word *surety*, simply stated in our language today, means a future guarantee. Proverbs 6:2 states, "Thou art snared with the words of thy mouth." Wow, what trouble we can get into with our mouths! How amazingly easy it is to simply say yes and then so quickly wish we hadn't. Sometimes a friend comes to us and says he or she needs money. If the money is for food or rent, of course we want to reach out to help as we are able. A good thing to do might be to invite your friend to eat with you. God clearly tells us this is what Jesus would do.

In this passage, however, we note there was a third party involved. This friend wanted a cosigner for something other than food. God is cautioning us here about business relationships with friends. The thought here is that we should keep healthy financial boundaries with friends. One thing is certain: there should be no money partnerships with friends (or others, for that matter). If they need resources, give them what you think is prudent. Also, you wouldn't want to turn a friendship into a creditor-debtor relationship. If a friend accuses you of being unloving because you don't loan him or her money, perhaps the best thing to say is, "Why don't you let me pray about that for a day or two." This gives us time to seek God for provision and wisdom, and it also gives the person who asked some time to rethink.

4. Stay Away from Idle People

> He that tilleth his land shall be satisfied with bread: but he that followeth vain persons is void of understanding. (Proverbs 12:11)

God states if we work hard, we will have plenty of bread, but perhaps not some high priced sushi roll (I would personally take the bread over the sushi anyway). Idle people have an agenda. Their goal is to have as much fun and avoid as much work as they can. I think one of the tragedies of modern culture is that we have developed a work-shy generation. Some parents, I think desiring to give their children the freedom they never had, will actually prohibit their young adult (ages fourteen to twenty-three) from working. The best thing we can do—for our sons especially—is to work the fire out of them. When you have one person who is idle, there is going to be some distress there. If you have a group of people who are idle and hang out together, that spells serious trouble.

5. True Friendships Are Based on Giving and not Getting

> The poor is hated even of his own neighbor but
> the rich hath many friends.(Proverbs 14:20)

God tells us that people who have money will soon find others interested in them. Not because of who they are but, rather, because of what they have. People who love stuff idolize people who have lots of stuff. I believe we should put friends in quotes here. Not real friends but convenient friends, who just care about riches. If we want to be a true friend to somebody, we must not care about how much money he or she has. We are to be givers—not someone obsessed with getting.

6. The Party Life Will Catch Up to You

> Be not among winebibbers ... (Proverbs 23:20)

Solomon is warning his son about alcohol. In today's culture, alcohol use is constantly growing. According to the November 2008 report By Rebecca Smith, Medical Editor for *The Telegraph*, alcohol consumption has doubled since the 1960's. That doesn't surprise me. Unbelievers are just trying to cover the emptiness. But what I wonder about are folks who make such a big case for Christians being able to drink alcohol. Why do they fight so hard for this? It seems to me it's not the grape juice they're interested in. Sounds to me they enjoy the buzz more than the grape juice! The issue here is about drinking to get a buzz. God pulls no punches when He states that wine abusers *shall* come to poverty. Whether it is the cost of the alcohol (at $1,000 a bottle trying to impress a girl) or a loss of financial discernment, alcohol is no friend to prosperity.

Let me close this chapter by quoting Jason Cabler of *Celebrating Financial Freedom*. Jason tells us how to know if you are broke. You know your broke if...

- ...If you find yourself googling "recipes for roadkill".

- ...If your tires are balder than your grandfather.

- ...If you're reusing your coffee grounds.

- ...If you have no change left under the couch cushions.

- ...You were escorted out of the KFC because you were licking other people's fingers.

- ...Your idea of feeding the poor is making yourself lunch.

- ...If you have seriously thought about selling the kids... or at least renting them out.

CHAPTER 2

Financial Wisdom Principle #2
Choose Wisdom

IT WOULD BE NICE if we didn't have to make decisions about money. Life would sure be easier if we didn't always have to worry about making ends meet. But God often uses our finances as a way of helping us discover real faith. One wonderful attribute of our God is that He is a loving and caring Father God, who does not leave us without a road map. He's not a detached deity, who tells us to get to a destination but leaves it to us to figure out how to get there. He gives us wise and clear directions in the Bible. The Bible is *the* book of wisdom.

What is wisdom? It's been defined in so many different ways. One author said wisdom is accumulated experience. That's why people sometimes say those with a gray head have lots of wisdom. Another author stated that wisdom is simply being enlightened. A Pastor said wisdom is using knowledge with common sense (I like that). One defined wisdom as truth coupled with action. Wisdom is all of these things … and more!

The Holy Spirit spoke through Solomon, who was called the wisest man who ever lived. The book of Proverbs was written not at the beginning but at the end of Solomon's life, after he went through a variety of experiences. The Holy Spirit allowed these experiences to be laid open for all humans of all generations to examine. He talks a lot about money. In fact, at least 150 verses in the book of Proverbs are about finances. Though Solomon had lots of money, he also had lots of questions and decisions to make about that money. Regardless of whether you feel like you have it all together financially, we can all use some sound advice. It has been said that money talks. American country music singer Joe Stampley said that if money talks, all mine says is, "Bye-bye."

1. Choose the High Priorities

> If thou seekest her as silver, and searchest for her
> as for hid treasures … (Proverbs 2:4)

If we count getting wisdom as high a priority as silver, God will bless us with true prosperity. We are to search for wisdom as we would for hidden treasure. The wisdom of God is truly better than any treasure.

> So that thou incline thine ear unto wisdom …
> (Proverbs 2:2)

This means we should welcome truth, to receive it—literally "to lean." I guess the question is which way are you leaning? Our financial health is about direction; God blesses direction. Sometimes we feel like we have to completely untangle the mess we have gotten ourselves into before God can bless us. But the truth is that God blesses wise direction even *before* we get to our desired locations.

Proverbs 3:14 states, "The merchandise of it is better than the merchandise of silver." Some of us love thrift store shopping, and others may like to go to swap meets. I don't guess there's anything quite so exciting than to find something for only a few dollars that's worth a lot more. But as exciting as that is, we should be looking for a good deal on wisdom. Notice how that God-inspired "intellectual property" is compared to actual money. I was listening to one of the leaders of Apple Corp. explain why they charge for the information they have. He called it "intellectual property." It wasn't free to come up with all those facts; it's a real commodity. We might think they should give it away. But if you really think about it, it cost Apple a pretty penny to come up with the information. Wisdom is real merchandise and very valuable. Someone may ask how much you made on a certain investment. We might have to say not much money but a lot of wisdom!

Years ago, in my early twenties, I made a "time-plan" purchase. We purchased a mobile home. The salesman we bought it from had a sign hanging in his office that read, "Kentucky Colonel." Intrigued, I asked him what the sign meant. He smugly said the award was given only to special people who had displayed exceptional honesty in their dealings. I took that in hook, line, and sinker. A few months later, when hidden costs started coming out of the woodwork, I realized just how naïve I had been. I learned a lot of wisdom!

2. Choose Effort

> Where no oxen are, the crib is clean: but much
> increase is by the strength of the ox. (Proverbs 14:4)

Life is full of stressful inconveniences. Most of us run from these, but there are unpleasant tasks that *are* necessary. I call them good stress. There is bad stress and then there is good stress. Good stress is the junk we must go through to accomplish something good.

Raising children is an example. It is possible to have a very clean house and less problems but then you miss the strength of having a family and people around you. Clean stables mean no workers; that's what the oxen were—hard workers. And, of course, no workers means no harvest, and no harvest means you will miss out on the resources God wants you to have.

Let me give you an example. If a husband and wife choose for her not to work outside the home, they have actually made one of the greatest steps toward financial freedom. Not surprisingly, however, most people would think that if you are going to make it in this world, you need two incomes from careers. Certainly there is nothing sinful about having a double (a triple, etc., for that matter) income. But a mother working full time outside the home can bring difficult issues.

The lack of Christian education for children would be one example of an issue to deal with. Many families have discovered that homeschooling allows them the time to invest truth into their children. They can build wisdom into their sons and daughters at times that are both planned and unplanned. One of my teenage daughters asked to be excused from the dinner table earlier than usual. Something didn't seem normal to me. After a few minutes, I walked into her bedroom. She was lying on her bed, reading her Bible. I sat down next to her and asked if something was wrong (she is quick to open up in her emotions). She shared a concern about friendships. We prayed together, and I left. That moment was possible because I was there. A parent who is available is a powerful tool for truth. God states that if you have to choose between a clean but empty stall and a messy but full one, choose the oxen!

Another great example of how a stay-at-home mom helps the family finances is that she can cook nutritious meals. Many people have a hard time affording health insurance. I bought membership at a local health club. As I worked out, I could sense I was getting healthier by the moment. Even though the monthly fee was an extra cost, I concluded it was a lot cheaper than full service health insurance! The same concept is true with the mother who is at home, can cook nutritious meals, and save money that might have been wasted on fast food.

Let's see what Proverbs 12:14 says: "A man shall be satisfied with good by the food of his mouth and the recompense [compensation, another financial term] of a man's hand shall be rendered unto him." God says there is always compensation ... there is always a payday. What we do with our hands and bodies is compensated. Parents may say the "tough" but needful choice was that they *had* to put their children in day care. But I urge readers to consider that the final payday on that decision may end up costing you much more than if a mother had avoided a career outside the home. Obviously, there are special circumstances, such as that of a single mom or disabled husband, where there is a need for a mother to have a full-time career outside the home.

3. Choose Love

> Better is a dinner of herbs where love is than a
> stalled ox and hatred therewith. (Proverbs 15:17)

Imagine you are biting into a big rib-eye steak ... so good and juicy! God states it would be better to just have a plate of herbs (like the kind of salad my wife likes) and love than a steak without peace in the home. This verse warns us about the high price of extravagance—the simple fact of paying more than you have to and the resulting emptiness it brings. God doesn't oppose quality … just wastefulness.

To pay more for something of equal quality just to gain status because it's a name brand is not worth it. Financial decisions often reveal our priorities. I heard of a rich man who had priority issues and wanted to take all his money with him when he died. He told his wife to collect all his money into a sack and hang it from the attic rafters. He said, "When my spirit is caught up into heaven, I will grab that sack on the way up and take it with me!" Well, when he finally died, his wife ran up to the attic, but that sack was still hanging where she had placed it. She said, "I knew I should've put the sack in the basement." Ouch!

Speaking about extravagance, there was a young man who had an accident in his beautiful car. When the police arrived, the officer overheard the young man mumbling near his car. The policeman walked closer to the young man and heard him clearly saying, "Oh my BMW, my BMW!" The policeman said, "Are you nuts? Look at your arm. It's all mangled!" The young man looked down at his arm and then cried, "Oh my Rolex!" Some things are of greater value than nice stuff … like good health!

The Bible was written thousands of years ago, yet its principles are ageless. In the early 2000s here in America, there were a lot of "stalled oxen" purchased. These "oxen" were actually expensive six- and seven-bedroom houses for just a mom, dad, two kids, and a dog. There were also large, gas-guzzling SUVs. One of the most common mistakes many Americans make is to spend more than they can afford on a home or vehicle. Christian financial authors Ron Blue, the late Larry Burkett, and Dave Ramsey all agree most Christians spend more than they should on their cars. I don't know what is so luring about overpriced cars, but Satan has a real stronghold in this area for most of us.

I see programs and books that state, "You can be rich!" The question I wonder is when and what qualifies a person to be classified as "rich"? Is it when you can have everything you want? That's impossible, because no one can ever get *everything* he or she wants at any given time. Over the years, the Lord has developed for me a definition of what a rich person is. *A rich person is one who wants everything he or she has!* On the other hand, a poor person wants everything he or she *doesn't* have. I knew a man who considered himself rich when he opened the refrigerator and saw it was full. He really didn't have much other than that. But he also didn't have debt. He always tithed and lived simply. For others, a full refrigerator is something they take for granted. They only feel rich when they have a certain amount of money in the bank.

God does not condemn those who may have more than the next person. But when money comes between my family and my faith, something is seriously wrong. Money actually equals *time*. When I buy something, it takes time. If that time always takes me away from my family, there needs to be some new priorities. We might come home with a new car but hear the children say, "I'd rather have an old car but more time with you." Stalled oxen are not worth it when there is no love.

4. Choose Balance

There is that maketh himself rich: yet hath nothing. (Proverbs 13:7)

What is God talking about in this verse? This Scripture doesn't seem to make sense at first glance. We make ourselves rich but have nothing? Are there really people who make themselves poor?

Choosing to be poor can actually be the wise choice at times. The warning here is about staying balanced. This truth is about not living above our means. Some people appear to be very rich, but if all their debts were paid, they'd be just like everyone else—or even less well off! This verse speaks of voluntarily making ourselves poor for a greater cause. It can be interpreted in two ways. First, giving your money away and investing in the kingdom of God. In this scenario, you've made yourself poor physically, but you have become spiritually rich. The second interpretation might be an acknowledgment that there are some people who live like old Scrooge and rob their family of what could be used for its benefit. That's what I mean by balance.

This brings up a question about standard of living. What should our standard of living be? If the Lord decides to bless us with extra, amen! Some of the richest people who have ever lived were also wonderful Christians. Solomon was perhaps the richest man who ever lived. There were also Job, Abraham, and David. They all had high standards of living. God is not against someone being rich. But I think it's important to understand that when God increases our resources, it's not His automatic green light to tell us to start spending. That is missing the point. Of course, there is nothing wrong with using our dollars on vacations, homes, and cars. After all, God is the one who created all of the lands and materials to enjoy! But I believe God has bigger plans for us than simply getting a nicer bed, better car, or going on a bigger vacation.

5. Choose Right

> Better is a little with righteousness than great
> revenues without right. (Proverbs 16:8)

Godly priorities are so important to our financial life. Better is little. Am I better off having less money? Sometimes actually yes! God doesn't say that's the way it *has* to be. He simply says if you *have* to choose, it's better to have little with a clear conscience than great revenues without doing right. It is better to do right, to love God, to serve God, to put our eyes on the Lord, and to have a very small estate. It's better for our family. It's better for our health. It's better for the kingdom of God.

When God speaks of choosing righteousness it might mean having to give up something. For example, many families have discovered that Christian education is the right thing for their family. Christian education, however, can be costly, even if it's home education. Choosing a righteousness education, therefore, may actually cost us. Another example might be choosing not have Mom work full time outside the home as discussed previously. We might be forced to do with less for a season.

Some people, as we all know, get income the wrong way. But we who are children of God must never compromise a scriptural truth or principle to make a buck. If I compromise the righteousness of God's Word to make a dollar, I have made the wrong choice. Choose right—always—and let God take care of the resources! Why is this so important? Let me give you one thought. We face some situations where the only thing that can help is God. In that moment, I want to know I'm right with God. I want to know I can get hold of God. If I have voluntarily placed myself in a needy position by doing the right thing, I can feel confident in coming to God and saying, "Lord, vindicate me, deliver me, help me in my time of need. Come to my aid." I can cry out! But if I've made unwise decisions and chosen the dollar over the glory of God, I don't feel like I can come to God.

Solomon tells us that our finances are always going to be changing, no matter who we are. Nobody ever has always has all they want. But God will eventually come to your aid – just choose the right thing and watch God work!

6. Choose the Simple Life

> Better it is to be of a humble spirit; [just a simple, quiet life with those that may not have all the names and the power or the influence] with the lowly than to divide the spoil with the proud. (Proverbs 16:19)

This is one principle the world around us will absolutely *never* understand. This world is trying to get all it can. God says the humble life is the desirable life, because God is attracted to humility. We become attractive person to God when we live a humble life. Did you know a humble life is actually attractive to everybody? The most beautifying makeup a woman can put on is a humble and grateful spirit. It's something money could certainly never buy! It's such a beautiful thing.

There's a story about a Swiss clockmaker who understood the value of the simple life. A certain group of people had gone in to see his beautiful craftsmanship, but they noticed it was taking him forever to make the clocks. They suggested that if he did this or that, he would make more money and faster. The Swiss man looked at them and said, "I don't make money; I make clocks!" It makes a whole lot of a difference when we know what we're going after. Of course, we need money to make ends meet for our family, and there's nothing wrong with that. God put that in us. But the healthy choice is to live humbly.

I close this chapter with a quote from an unknown source on *Proverbia*. "Here's what money will buy: money will buy a bed but not sleep, books but not brains, food but not an appetite, a house but not a home, medicine but not health, amusement but not happiness, finery but not beauty, a crucifix but not a savior." Let's get our priorities right!

In the next chapter, we talk about discerning what true success is. Solomon was concerned about being a successful man, but how can we know what true success is?

CHAPTER 3

Financial Wisdom Principle #3
Discern True Success

LARRY BURKETT IN HIS great book *Using Your Money Wisely* says one out of every five things Jesus talked about, as recorded in the New Testament, actually concerns success with our money or possessions. Why? Because our Savior knew it was absolutely impossible to divorce our spiritual life from our financial life. In fact, in Luke 16, it states that if you know how to handle your money, God can trust you with true spiritual riches. That's what I want!

What is success? American educator Marva Collins stated that success doesn't come to you; you go to it. Success is on purpose, whether it be a successful relationship or successful finances. Vince Lombardi said if we chase perfection, we can catch excellence. Success really is about the character we possess.

Now let's examine what true success is.

1. Success Is Living Long

> Length of days is in her right hand. (Proverbs 3:16)

The "her" in this verse means wisdom. The verse before it reads, "And in her left hand, riches and honor." Solomon said he saw wisdom coming at him with arms wide open. And while the length of days was in her right hand, there was something else in her left hand-long life. Biblical Hebrew culture says that whatever is in the right hand is the most important. As good as riches and honor are, that which is in the right hand—long life—is even better! Sometimes we wonder, *A long life? Are we talking about chronological days?* Of course that would be part of it, but the actual word *long* would more likely mean "full" or "fulfilled." So what we're talking about here is having your days *filled* with joy, *filled* with peace, and *filled* with the blessings of God.

We know it is possible to have money and yet be unable to really enjoy it. We can acquire something we really like-such as big boat- and then put an exorbitant amount of money into it and then find we're "enjoying" it so much that it might be short-changing the balance of our lives.

Some people actually live twice as long in half the time, because they've lived a full life. Some people will testify that once they get right with God, the skies get a little more blue and the trees are a little more beautiful. A holy life helps me to really enjoy everything. The full life will be a blessed life. It's a life that is not broken through misspent days. Rather, it is fixed and functions well. I once read that a certain fellow was talking about his "fixed" income. He was a senior man in age. A younger man said to him, "It must be nice having a fixed income." The older man surmised, "Fixed income ... mine is more like broken." True success is living a fixed life!

2. Success Is Choosing to Have Godly Honor

> Exalt her and she shall promote thee, she shall bring thee to honor when thou dost embrace her. (Proverbs 4:8)

Godly honor and true success go together. True success is being a person with integrity; that is, when our words and actions match up. In a world that's in a hot pursuit of worldly success, finding people who have godly honor and real integrity is becoming more and more rare.

Why would godly honor be of such high value? Why would it be the godly way of defining success? This world's definition of success is to go a large, metro-area, five-star hotel and listen to beautiful people speak about winning. There is a good chance you'll not find them saying godly honor is the way to be successful.

Why is honor so important? Are we talking about fame? No. We have seen some of these crazy reality-show people imagine they are stars, because everyone knows about them. But godly honor is something far different than popularity. Honor allows me to be an influencer. Everyone influences somebody. When you have honor, people can trust you, and when they trust you, they are moved to action. We can then leave a legacy of touching lives for Christ.

3. Success Is Being Content with Who We Are

> He that is despised, and hath a servant, is better than he that honoureth himself, and lacketh bread. (Proverbs 12:9)

Godly contentment is not complacency. We can't afford to ever get satisfied and stop growing. But being who we are means we are able to accept our condition and whatever limitations, and make the best life of it. "He that is despised [this is talking about someone with limited resources] and hath a servant [but is able to enjoy common conveniences, such as having a servant], is better than he that honoreth himself and lacketh bread." A good present-day example might be to tell you of the time I was visiting in a beautiful large home. It was in the middle of the summer, and *inside* their house, it must have been in the nineties! I think they could see I was melting. They offered an apology. "Oh sorry. We can't afford the electric bill." That, to me, is an example of someone who honors themselves by trying to "impress the Jones" with this giant home, yet is not able to afford air-conditioning! Maybe if they had a smaller house, they might have been able to afford some cooling.

Another example might be "name-brand-itis." It's a sickness that often tempts all of us. I was reading about the entrance regulations to Harvard University. Many parents work hard to save money so their children can have a college education—but not just any college, the best! We want Harvard! According to *The Ivy Coach* for the Class of 2015, 34,950 students applied to Harvard College and 2,158 students were admitted, representing only 6.2% of the applicant pool. Of those who applied approximately 3,800 applicants were ranked first in their high school classes. More than 14,000 applicants scored 700 or above on the SAT Critical Reading test, 17,000 scored 700 or above on the SAT Math test, and 15,000 scored 700 or higher on the SAT Writing test. Wow! Does this mean the other students are destined to live a terrible life, because they did not have the esteem of a Harvard education? No. I think you can go on to live a happy life without going to Harvard. I heard Dave Ramsey say that we often spend money we haven't even earned yet to buy things we don't even need to impress people we don't even know! God is reminding us that true success is being who we are.

4. True Success Is about Having Genuine Joy

> Treasures of wickedness profit nothing. (Proverbs 10:2)

When you have real joy—that's success! God states you can get treasures through worldly measures, but it won't bring true peace. You can, on occasion, become rich doing things that are not right. God isn't saying that wrong ways don't make money at times. But does it really profit in the end? No, "righteousness delivereth from death" (Proverbs 10:2). Living right can literally keep you from dying. Crime doesn't pay if you're dead. And there is more than one way to be dead. We're talking here about soul death here—the heart (Proverbs 10:3). Many people are *alive,* but they're not *living,* because their heart is dead. They have no joy, no fun, no excitement; they're just going through the motions.

God wants us to have a soul that's fat not famished, a soul that is full, "but he casteth away the substance of the wicked" (Proverbs 10:4). Count on it. If you make money the wrong way, it will eventually go bye-bye! It will disappear in the end of our lives, of course, but often before our final days. One of the most challenging financial tasks for Christians is to make wise investments in a morally responsible way. Instead of investing, some people practice "sin-vesting." Sin-vesting often gives the highest return in the market. There's even one financial planning company called Vice X. They deal with financial products for things having to do with vices. Their stocks were in the top-ten performing stocks. However, sin-vesting will not profit in the end, because we lose peace of mind. God says it's not worth it. It's better to have only 10K with spiritual joy than to have 20K with no peace. I believe before we invest we should ask ourselves, "Does it involve abortion, alcohol, drugs, porno, or gambling?" I personally would never want to knowingly allow the money God gave me go to promote immorality.

I read a story this week about a very wealthy man, who definitely didn't need pocket change, walk along the street and pick up all the coins he saw. After picking them up, he examined them. One person who saw him was amazed he took his time doing this. At first he thought, *This man loves money so much he is searching for pennies!* Finally, he asked the man, "You certainly don't need the money. Why do you search for coins and examine them before putting them into your pocket?" The man replied, "You know why I do that? I pick up that penny and read where it says 'In God We Trust.' Then I say to myself "God is my supplier." I worship and praise Him. And then I put the money in my pocket."

5. Success Is Having a Virtuous Mate

> A virtuous woman is a crown to her husband: but she that maketh ashamed is as rottenness in his bones. (Proverbs 12:4)

What is a virtuous woman? Among other things, she is a woman who has a kind and godly tongue, a keeper at home, supports and follows the leadership of her husband, and has a positive attitude. We are told that "she is a crown." That is, she is priceless! God says a man who has a virtuous wife may not have millions, but he is as rich as a king. A godly husband is a great treasure to his wife as well.

Proverbs 19:14 states, "House and riches are the inheritance of fathers: and a prudent wife is from the Lord." A prudent wife is from the Lord. That doesn't mean a prude! It is, rather, a discerning mate. This verse tells me God is the divine matchmaker. God is in the business of putting people together. A man might think he picked a woman, but God works through circumstances, and as much as we think it's up to us, it's much more due to the Lord's touch.

What is the value of a wife or mother? We all know raising children has an incredible impact on society. The greatest job in America is being a mother. They are at the core of society. They hold in their hands these little children. It's an incredible job! What is the worth of a mother? *Salary.com* released their annual market evaluation of mother's work. They talked to four hundred stay-at-home moms and identified ten major jobs a mother does and the hours she typically spends doing those jobs. They tried to evaluate how much they would have to pay someone to do that job if they were to hire the jobs. They determined a stay-at-home mother averages about ninety-two hours a week. They perform jobs such as housekeeping, cooking, cleaning, janitorial, day-care keeper, CEO, manager and facility manager. *Salary.com* said their worth is approximately $134,121. You would have to hire someone for that amount to do a mother's job. Thank God for godly mates!

6. Successes Are Lips of Knowledge

> There is gold, and a multitude of rubies: but the lips of knowledge are a precious jewel. (Proverbs 20:15)

It is easy to find someone who wears jewels, but to find someone who wears a godly attitude and has kind words is very rare.

Anyone can buy jewels, but not everyone have lips of knowledge; it is a genuine jewel. Lips of knowledge are pleasant and considerate. They are careful about what they choose to say. Lips of knowledge have been such a blessing to me personally over the years. People who know things can be very helpful in our time of need.

Let me share a personal experience. Years ago, I heard someone say one way to save money on a large purchase might be to become an actual "dealer" of that product. When it came time to build our first church building, I remembered that concept. I was praying one early morning, and God seemed to tell me to look into becoming a metal building dealer. As soon as 8:00 a.m. came, I called a company to ask if they were looking for any metal building dealers. I told him our church had a gentleman who was a general contractor who might be interested. The company put me in touch with the district manager for our area, and by the end of the day, the district manager, the contractor, and I were meeting together to discuss the details of becoming a metal building distributor. We ended up saving $40,000 by becoming a dealer! Those lips of knowledge someone gave us turned into a huge savings on our part.

> A word fitly spoken is like apples of gold in pictures of silver. (Proverbs 25:11)

People who know to say the right thing at the right time, to give good counsel or instruction, are a huge benefit to our lives.

7. Success Is Truth

> Buy the truth, and sell it not. (Proverbs 23:23)

Never sell out! Whatever truth costs or whatever it requires, do it. Do not ever sell out. God wants us to hold onto truth. Why is truth so important? It's important because there is no success without truth. It's just like success in a relationship. If people lie to each other, you cannot have a good relationship. There's always going to be something between you. In relationships, it is so important to have truth, to lay it all out on the table. Talk and get all the truth out. It's a sad thing when we no longer have truth.

I recently read the story of the famous musician Elton John. He is not a very moral man. He lives a perverted lifestyle and has done tremendous harm with his immoral lyrics and the lifestyle he promotes. I read, however, that he was raised in a religious home. Typical of many of secular singers today, he got his start in church! The church provides an opportunity and an atmosphere for them to hone their skills. As he grew up though, he sold out. He sold out the truth. He has money, but he doesn't have true success. He lives a lie, because he sold out what he once had. God wants us to hold onto truth.

Proverbs 24:4 says, "And by knowledge shall thy chambers be filled with all precious and pleasant riches." It's been said that if you give someone a meal, the person will have food for an hour. But if you give an individual a shovel, he or she will have food for a week. Help people understand how to get money rather than hand them money. Turn truth into a real source of income. I read about a man who found out quite by accident that used coffee grounds burn. He threw his spent grounds into a little can and let them dry out. He'd throw those dried-out grounds into the fireplace—instant fire! He began to wonder if he could make any logs out of the grounds. He went to his garage, melted some wax, and mixed it with the coffee grounds. He tried the log in his fireplace. It burned just like the little wood logs you can get at a store. This man told someone about it, and now his company, Java Logs, has sold millions! It's amazing how a little knowledge can turn into great riches.

8. Success Is a Clear Conscience

> He that covereth his sins shall not prosper. (Proverbs 28:13)

God doesn't mind us being prosperous; we just have to define "prosperity" correctly. If you cover your sins, you'll never prosper! On the other hand, "whoso confess and forsaketh them shall have mercy." It is so foolish to rationalize and excuse our mistakes or errors. If we are human, we are bound to make mistakes. As husbands, wives, children, fathers, mothers, humans, and Christians, we *will* sin. I remember hearing E. V. Hill, the great African American pastor from Southern California say about Pastors and their personal lives (at a time when several well-known TV ministers were falling into sin, and all sorts of issues were surfacing) "E. V. Hill sins too... I am not a perfect man." I remember hearing that and saying to myself, "Yes, He's so right!" We point our fingers at those men with big names who are falling, but the truth is, we *all* sin. None of us does it all right—*none* of us. So what do we do when we sin? We have such a tendency to cover it. But God says if you cover it, you'll not prosper.

We must make it right. Even saying "sorry" can turn into a saving of thousands. There's a new movement called Sorry Works. The man started it after a physician botched the diagnosis of his brother, and he died. But when the truth came out, the doctor and his staff ran from the family. They wouldn't talk to them in the hospital or anywhere. It's human nature, of course, to pull back when you've blown it. They also knew anything they said might be used against them in court. However, the fellow was just so put off by all the arrogance. All they would have had to say is, "Hey, we blew it. How can we make it right?" The founders of Sorry Works believe they can save millions of dollars a year in physician insurance premiums if they are just willing to admit fault, face up to their actions, and try to make things right.

9. Success Is God-Blessed Resources

Not all money is created equal. Hold up two $10 bills. Now they may look the same, but one has a blessing on it, and the other doesn't.

> The blessing of the Lord, it maketh rich, and he addeth no sorrow with it. (Proverbs 10:22)

Take the money out of your wallet and question it. Does it have the blessing of the Lord on it? I don't want any sorrow with that $20 bill! If there's any sorrow attached to it, I don't want it. I want His blessing on it. God says it takes His blessing on our finances for us to be able to enjoy them. God gives us 9 key principles in Proverbs to get His favor on our money. Whether it be $5, $10, or $1,000, it needs to have His blessing so we can enjoy it. If our finances aren't blessed, God says all kinds of trouble will be associated with them. No matter how much we may have it will never be enough without the blessing of the Lord.

A story is told about two old friends who bumped into each other on the street one day. One of them looked forlorn, almost on the verge of tears. His friend asked him, "What happened to you?" His friend replied, "Let me tell you. My uncle died a few weeks ago and left me $40,000, and then a cousin died just a few days ago and left me $80,000, free and clear!" The other friend asked, "What's the problem? You sound like you have been blessed!" His friend interrupted, "You don't understand. Last week my great aunt passed away, and I inherited almost a quarter of a million dollars!" Now he was really confused. He asked why he was so glum then. The friend replied, "This week I inherited nothing!" It's never enough!

CHAPTER 4

Financial Wisdom Principle #4
Learn Contentment

AREN'T WE GLAD WE can look to what the Bible says about financial matters? My spirit tells me one thing, and flesh says another. But then I look at the Word of God, and I know what is really true! Knowing and doing, however, is another story.

This is especially true concerning our personal finances. As we attempt to apply biblical principles, sometimes our circumstances, cultures, and traditions keep us from doing what the Lord asks us to do. For example, the Bible says that if we want to be blessed, we will give 10 percent of our gross income to the Lord's work. This has been a biblical pattern for over six thousand years, yet our minds remind us of a thousand reasons why we can't.

We are not alone. Solomon said he had often missed peace and contentment because of his inordinate desire to get things he didn't have. One of life's greatest treasures is the ability to be content without being complacent. God has put within us a desire to achieve and gain things. That's not bad, but he wants us to learn contentment *while* we're trying to get ahead. Let's do a little review here. In the first chapter, we discussed destructive influences. I am amazed at how often we have to watch out for financial schemes. The second chapter spoke of maintaining the right priorities. It is impossible to have a good financial life without prioritizing. In the third chapter, it was discerning what true success is; if we discern true success, we can then achieve it. This chapter is about learning contentment. It's not something we are born with.

When we don't have contentment and our hearts are filled with greed, there is nothing in this world that can satisfy us. Greed is a terrible thing. As we talk about the symptoms of greed, we'll discover there are red flags. We'll learn to recognize that greed is just a symptom of a far deeper problem.

1. A Symptom of Greed Is When People Get in a Hurry

> So are the ways of every one that is greedy of gain,
> which taketh away the life of the owners thereof.
> (Proverbs 1:19)

We're going to get money, and we're going to get it now! Gain is not wrong; profit is not wrong. God never chastises us for making a profit. But being greedy of gain is far different. The Bible says it, "takes away the life of the owners thereof." When we're greedy of money, regardless of what it takes to get it, God says it, "takes away the life." Greed steals fulfillment and takes away our sense of contentment. God says if you're greedy of gain, you're really *not* going to get what you hoped for. We gain a new understanding of that little phrase, "making a killing on a deal." We'll make a killing all right—we kill our own spirit!

Proverbs 28:20 states something similar, only in a little bit more positive way: "A faithful man shall abound with blessings but he that maketh haste to be rich shall not be innocent." In all likelihood, a person who just has to be rich and have it now is likely to fall into some illegal, immoral, or unethical behaviors. It is not wrong to be quick in the sense of being efficient. Being efficient is good. But this verse refers to people who need to get rich now, regardless of breaking God's rules or laws.

Trying to get rich quickly makes us gullible. We have all seen those ads that promise, "Own business," or, "Work from home." I've seen signs around town that read, "I retired at 39!" and, "Make $1,000 in minutes!" People claim they make thousands of dollars, while wearing their pajamas and sitting on the couch. I will tell you right now that 99 percent of those "opportunities" are scams! Occasionally, you will find somebody who has a legitimate business and sells legitimate goods. They are blessings to people and really do make a living from doing things on the Internet. I know a man, for example, who buys and sells on Craigslist. He took some seed money, about $1,000, and spends time combing the Craigslist ads, gets a really good deal, and then turns it around and sells it back on Craigslist for a small profit. He often makes a few extra dollars a week that way. That's a legitimate way to work from home. But to think we're going to sit at home in our underwear and be able to kick our feet up on the table and make thousands of dollars without effort? It just doesn't work that way.

2. Another Symptom of Greed Is Hoarding

> He that withholdeth corn, the people shall curse him: but blessing shall be upon the head of him that selleth it. (Proverbs 11:26)

This is the pack rat mentality. We had a hamster, which someone gave us (people have always given us little critters). One day we put some cotton into his cage, thinking he would have a nice place to lay his furry little body. We came in sometime later, and the cotton was gone! The children asked, "Where did all the cotton go?" I looked at Mr. Furball, and he looked like he had mumps! The little guy had stuffed the cotton into his cheeks. Now that's a hoarder! We sometimes do that as humans, and when you look at our cheeks—that is, our closets or garages. They are bulging.

Hoarding is a problem. It is an issue for companies as well as individuals. You may have heard the true story about the Collier brothers from several years ago. They were found deceased in their large New York City home. These reclusive men were found amid a hundred tons of junk! Magazines, newspapers, and everything you can think of—they had never thrown away anything.

Hoarding can be very compulsive behavior. Some can't even throw away a newspaper, because some piece of information is going to "change their life" someday! Other folks can't put things away in drawers, because they think they'll forget they have it if they can't see it. Their lives become cluttered. Others stockpile, perhaps to drive the market in lean times through price gouging. God says there is a special favor, a blessing, on kind businesspeople. When we do business deals, it ought to be a win-win situation.

This does bring up a bigger issue: why does God give us resources? Are resources to be protected at any cost? Reasonable protection is well and good, but resources are to be seen as a reserve, a ready reserve hopefully, in case something happens in our lives. There was no such thing as insurance companies in Solomon's day. Lands, possessions, or cash were the only insurance there was. Sometimes situations arose necessitating the sale of your resources or using your cash.

The way I look at it is this: when I die, if I have a few dollars, fine. If I don't, that's fine, too. What I want is to do the right thing every day. No matter what that means, I want to do the right thing for God and my family, every single day—the right thing with my resources and my life. Hoarding attempts to conserve what God calls us to use.

3. A Symptom of Greed Is Loving Pleasure at Any Cost

> He that loveth pleasure shall be a poor man:
> he that loveth wine and oil shall not be rich.
> (Proverbs 21:17)

No doubt about that! God then gives an example: "He that loveth wine and oil shall not be rich." This clearly points out that if we are in love with wine (things that we taste), oil (things that we use to make us beautiful), the good life (eating and drinking), and things to make us look nice, we shall not be rich. It's going to end up eating away at our resources. Does this mean we can't enjoy nice food? Of course not. God that gave us taste buds. It was God who told us to richly enjoy all things. Should we try to look better? Yes. I think to some degree, we should do our best to better ourselves.

Women ask, "Should a Christian woman wear makeup?" The old evangelist used to say, "Well, when I was growing up on the farm, when the barn needed painting, you painted it!" God isn't against us looking nice or enjoying food, but if we "love" and set our hearts on it at any cost, there is a problem.

I believe this brings up a point about expensive hobbies. One thing that takes an elephant bite out of our finances is an expensive hobby. As a young adult, I loved golf (I still think it's the greatest sport in the world ... I love it ... it's a great combination of sport and recreation). But golf can be *very* expensive. It was expensive years ago, and it's even more expensive now. When you really get into golf, you want to visit different courses. Playing these courses can become pricey. Then, of course, we want the finest equipment—and golfers, you know how we are. We must have the fanciest and biggest toys we can find. We're not content with a driver from five years ago; we have got to have Big Big Bertha. As a young father, I soon discovered that between the time and cost, this hobby was simply not going to work for me.

Let's list a few hobbies that can get very expensive. Collecting anything is usually very expensive. Then there is travel. Oh my goodness—traveling! If you love expensive vacations, you *will* go broke! Traveling is actually strange to me. For example, we will travel halfway around the world to see the way people live and explore the "culture". If you want culture and you live in America today just look around, there are often a lot of "foreign" cultures right next door available for a whole lot less outlay!

Many people have found you can enjoy simple pleasures, like culinary pastimes, and not spend nearly as much money. It may take a little bit of extra time, but it's worth learning the craftsmanship.

4. Another Symptom of Greed Is Spending More than We Make

> There is treasure to be desired and oil in the dwelling of the wise; but a foolish man spendeth it up. (Proverbs 21:20)

It is stated, "a foolish man spendeth it up." Notice the word *spend*. We have to spend! But spending can become an addictive behavior. God gives us wisdom to live within our means. God gives us the basics—the simple things, the oil. He says to be content with the basics and thankful for the gravy.

There are a lot of vices that can blow our budget. Out of the top four vices that can blow your money, smoking is number one. A pack of cigarettes is very expensive. The price of a pack of cigarettes is always on the increase. *Better Health Channel* in November of 2012 stated that smoking costs money as well as your health. Cigarettes are expensive. Quitting can save you money now and future health costs too. If you smoke one pack of cigarettes each day for ten years, you'll spend enough money to buy a new car! Shopping can be another expensive vice. *World Psychiatry,* official journal of the World Psychiatric Association states that nearly 6% of the population is affected with compulsive buying disorder-this is no laughing matter!

Cell phones can also consume much of your money if you're not keeping an eye on them. It's amazing how quickly those minutes can add up. Americans go crazy over Lotto jackpots! The cruel truth about lotteries is however that they are a punitive tax on the poor and uneducated people who are the most avid buyers. A *Business Insider* article states that "The people who can least afford it are throwing away on average 47 cents on the dollar every time they buy a ticket.

And the government, which relies increasingly on the lottery for funding, goes out of its way to tell them it is a good idea".

5. Another Symptom of Greed Is Laboring to Be Rich

> Labour not to be rich: cease from thine own
> wisdom. (Proverbs 23:4)

Many students that I have asked the question, "What are you trying to get from your education?" answer, "To make money." However, God says to labor *not* to be rich. God's Word states the exact opposite of what so many people say today. Go to many financial seminars, and you will hear, "You can be rich!" My friend, that is a lie. God only promises to give us oil and bread. We will have enough to be healthy and get by. But become rich? Only a fraction of the population will ever accomplish that. If God builds up our estate through our diligence, praise God! As I've mentioned before, some of the most spiritual people in the Bible were those with substantial substance. Job was a "perfect man," yet he was rich and famous, and he worked hard six days a week. But what God is primarily warning about here are workaholics who want to be rich, regardless the cost.

6. Another Symptom of Greed Is Having an "I" Problem

> Wilt thou set thine eyes upon that which is not?
> for riches certainly make themselves wings; they fly
> away as an eagle toward heaven. (Proverbs 23:5)

We're not talking about needing glasses here! We're talking about being caught by the "eye." It's okay to look at a house or a car and admire its look. But when we set our eyes on it, that's another story! How many of us can testify to this verse? We can so easily get self-consumed and miserable. Chuck Norris once said "Some of the most miserable people I know are some of the richest people in America".

Solomon says, "Riches certainly make themselves wings." The stuff money buys so soon passes away. There once was a sixteen-year-old young man who went shopping with his father. The son saw a beautiful computer system and said to his dad, "Dad, let's get that! We can afford it!" The dad looked at his son and asked, "*We* can afford it? *We*? *I* can afford it, but I don't want to do it. *You* can't afford it; you don't have the money." If we let our eyes get set upon something, you will often not only spend the money you have in hand, but you will spend the money you haven't even earned yet by putting that item on credit. God warns us about putting our eyes on things.

7. Another Symptom of Greed Is that It Is Never Satisfied

> The full soul loatheth an honeycomb; but to the hungry soul every bitter thing is sweet. (Proverbs 27:7)

Hunger is the best appetizer. We'd better learn how to be satisfied with whatever the Lord gives us. Having contentment is simply saying to others and God, "I need nothing to make me happy." If you can be happy just the way you are, you are content.

Remove far from me vanity and lies: give me neither poverty nor riches; feed me with food convenient for me: (Proverbs 30:8)

We must not misunderstand true value. The writer Agur prayed to the Lord to remove the emptiness and worldly lies syndrome. He said he'd lived long enough to understand the balance between value and cost. Sometimes things do cost more but are of better value. Sometimes things cost a lot but are of lesser value. He was just asking for a proper understanding of value. He's not looking for riches at any cost, and not necessarily trying to be poor, but asks for what would be best.

If you have nine children, as I do, you're going to need more resources than a family with one. It's the fact of greater needs. Solomon explains why he is looking for neither riches nor poverty: "Lest I be full and deny thee." Proverbs 30:9 It's so tempting when we have lots of resources to actually deny God. We don't think we need God. On the other hand, it's tempting if we're poor to steal and to hurt the name of God. Solomon is saying that he knows himself well enough to determine that if he was too rich, he'd forget God, and if too needy, he might be tempted to steal to make ends meet.

8. A Symptom of Greed Is that We Never Learn when Enough Is Enough

> The righteous eateth to the satisfying of his soul but the belly of the wicked shall want.
> (Proverbs 13:25)

Greedy people miss out on life, because they constantly have to have more. John D. Rockefeller once said, "This poorest person I know is the one who has nothing but money." Worldly people miss out on peace, because they always "need" more.

We might think a rich person is happy, because he or she doesn't appear to have needs. But it doesn't work that way.

Multimillionaire Ross Perot talked about why super-rich people are seldom happy. He said it's because rich people have more "stuff" and that more "stuff" breaks. Something is always broken on their yacht, on their private jet, even on their "stuff"; their "stuff" has issues. Enough should be enough.

CHAPTER 5

Financial Wisdom Principle #5
Manage Well

THERE IS A GREAT need in our homes and churches today to get back to the basics. This is certainly true in doctrinal issues. But this is also true in loving and living out the Word of God. I think one of the areas we need to rethink as believers are our finances.

Why does God give hundreds of financial principles in Scripture? Are they just a test to see how good we are? Is God just waiting to see if we go past a line and then will say to us, "I got you"? Absolutely not. God doesn't give us things because we *can't* do them. He gives us these truths because we *can* ... and they will be a tremendous benefit to us if, by the grace of God, we follow them.

If you live in America, you live in affluence, regardless of your current circumstances. There has never been any country in the history of humankind with more widespread opportunities than the United States during the twenty-first century. Never has there been any group of people with so much. And yet, despite our resources as Americans, we have built our lives around debt, especially over the past sixty years. Debt financing, however, is a foundation of sand. The cycles of recession and the financial fiascos we've experienced as a nation should not come as a surprise. They are largely the result of debt. They're going to keep happening as long as we borrow from the future. In contrast, the Word of God is a foundation of rock. When we build our life and finances on the Bible, we have staying power.

In this chapter, we talk about managing money. Even as rich as Solomon was, he still had to manage his money. Sometimes we think management is only necessary if you don't have much, but it is wise for all. It is always a challenge to get and keep your finances orderly. Money creates worries. One man said, "I never worry about money. I have enough to last me the rest of my life unless I buy something." I think we all can identify with that. One couple decided it was time to get their budgets in order. She had been working on the budget all night. He was watching television, and his wife came in and said, "Well, honey, I have worked on the budget. Now you work out getting a raise." She'd gotten things figured out! So he gave it a try and worked on it the next day. He then went to his wife and said, "Well, honey, I've worked it out and need a little help from you. I've figured out what we'll need for clothing, food, and shelter. We have a choice of any two of those."

What is managing well? What does it mean to plan our spending? It could be simply defined as applying godly discipline to our financial life, using biblical restraint and discernment. It is clear from Scripture that God does not demand one level of lifestyle from everybody. He is not a cookie-cutter God; He does not require every person to do things the same way. I'm sure God allows Christians to be across every strata of affluence. Some Christians are well-to-do and travel in circles with those of considerable resources. Others live more modestly. But all of us need a budget.

This chapter is about how to spend money wisely. We have spoken about being alert to destructive influences. What is the strongest protection we have for keeping our lives in order? That is to purposefully follow the Bible. If we are purposing to obey Scripture no matter what, it allows us to take time to think, pray, and make good decisions. We must maintain the right priorities. We take a huge step toward financial freedom when we decide to put God first. Then we discerned what true success is. God's view of success is different than our view of success. We have also discussed contentment. Don't spoil today by constantly looking at tomorrow. Remember, God has given us everything we need to be happy. If we're not happy now, we won't be happy a year from now or ten years from now. And we discuss managing well. Every family should visualize how God wants them to use the resources He's entrusted to them in the best possible way. There needs to be a clear plan. This means six things.

1. Use Our Estates for God

> Honour the Lord with thy substance, and with the
> firstfruits of all thine increase: (Proverbs 3:9)

First of all, it means to use our estates for God. Our estate is whatever we have. It can be an old minivan, a home, a 1958 Volkswagen (like me), or money in the bank. Or you may be blessed with a nice home to live in or have a stable financial portfolio. Whatever we possess, God wants us to use our estates for Him. Always honor the Lord with your substance. The ultimate goal of everything is to honor God. These hands and eyes were made to glorify God. This body was made to glorify God. I often pray, "God, help me to be your hands, your feet, and your arms today." Everything we do should be to glorify God.

The same is true about our assets; our possessions are to be used to glorify God. When one person really begins to glorify God with his or her substance, it is a beautiful thing! Look what happened in the New Testament when Barnabas (he was named right; he was an "encourager") sold his land and gave the money to God. The early church was going through a great spiritual revival, and when he plopped down tens of thousands of dollars at the apostle's feet, it ignited this young church. Barnabas's gift became a catalyst for further revival. Everybody knows that when you get your money in order, something good will happen.

God promises He will supply all our needs. As a young pastor, I tried to figure out exactly what a "need" was. I can go to God, pray, and be confident He will supply all my needs. The Bible guarantees that. So what is a need? One pastor said, "A need is anything I can use for God's glory." I love that definition! "Honour the Lord with thy substance." Can you honor God with what you're praying about? Then it's good.

Let me identify some things that might be considered a little extravagant in the eyes of some people, and yet, they can used for God. I've seen people use their boats or vacation homes for God's glory, allowing spiritual retreats perhaps. I've seen people use their hobbies for God. There are those who own horses and allow Sunday school children to come out and ride. I've also seen people use swimming pools for God's glory. I've seen people use large estates for God's glory. I've seen people use planes for God's glory. Riding in a small plane during foggy conditions is definitely a deeply spiritual time … I know.

2. Be Faithful to all Obligations

> Withhold not good from them to whom it is due,
> when it is in the power of thine hand to do it.
> (Proverbs 3:27)

What does managing well mean? It means being faithful to all obligations, big or small. Obligations are a part of life; they range from utilities to doctor bills, from cell phones to business contracts we enter into. Here's what it says in Proverbs 3:27: "Withhold not good." Withhold not good that is payment or money; don't hold onto the payment when it's due. When it's due, it's due! There are extending circumstances, of course, as Scripture is so wise to indicate. The last part of that verse states, "when it's in the power of thine hand to do it." Sometimes we enter into obligations that are not debts, and we have every good intention to pay. Everything looks in order to be able to take care of those payments, but sometimes, since we can't know the future, things happen. If it's a necessary obligation that's entered into in a scriptural way and you just can't fulfill it, you shouldn't walk around acting like you're on your way to hell because you are late on your payment. Handle it maturely … go and talk to the people. The Bible reminds us we must be faithful to our obligations.

This verse reminds us there are some who play games with their money. Don't say to your neighbor, "Go, and come again, and tomorrow I will it to you," when you have it now. Sometimes God lays upon your heart a burden to give to somebody. Let's not make them beg us; don't make them come back to you two or three times. Simply give, and don't make a big deal of it.

I believe this also refers to paying compensation without delay. If someone works for you, you need to pay that person. In the Scripture, people would often worked for a day and get paid at the end of the day. They were day laborers. If they do the work right now, it is good to pay them right now. The Bible talks of not "muzzling oxen that are treading out corn." I don't think the ox wants to wait thirty days to eat; it wants to eat right then! So we certainly ought to take care of people who work for us.

I learned a bitter but very valuable lesson years ago. I was going to Bible college and had started a window cleaning business. God blessed me in my own business for about two years before I went on staff at a large church. I had a "huge" capital investment of a squeegee, pole, bucket, and a sponge. But because I was now going into the ministry, I sold the business, that is, the clientele. A fellow came along and wanted to buy my business from me. This "Christian" man wrote me a check. I was so excited! This was a real answer to prayer. I took the check to the bank and found the account was closed. I figured something must be mistaken. After about a week, I was getting nervous. I finally got hold of him several weeks later and … well, you know the rest of the story, right? Never got a dime … only a piece of paper. How painful it is when we don't honor our word!

3. Make the Best of What You Have

> Much food is in the tillage of the poor, but there is that is destroyed for want of judgment. (Proverbs 13:23)

Wait a second ... there are some who say, "I can't do anything with $20!" You'd be surprised at what you could do with $20, $50, or $100. Some people can take $100 and make $1,000 out of it. It's really incredible! We can have less, but if we are industrious and thoughtful, God blesses what we have. "But there is that which is destroyed from lack of judgment." The word *judgment* here actually means "management." There are those with six-figure salaries but just cannot seem make it on that. Some wives have husbands who bring home a handsome income and yet they still feel insecure. That is because he has not shown himself to have wise judgment. If we work, pray, and manage well, God multiplies the resources. We should use and get the most of what we do have.

Ron Blue, in his book *Master Your Money* states what the top three money mistakes are. First and foremost, he stated it is a "consumptive lifestyle." I agree absolutely. The first and greatest financial mistake we Christians make is spending too much. The highest priority for these believers is to have the comforts of life. They will spend whatever it takes to make them feel good. And if they have anything left, they will either save it or maybe give a little to God. A consumptive lifestyle has serious consequences.

I was recently in a jewelry shop, getting a ring sized, and there was a young man who appeared to be in his twenties. He was looking at Rolex watches ... you know, Rolex watches; even the less-expensive ones can be three or four thousand dollars!

The man running the shop began talking about Mercedes and other expensive items. I had to laugh to myself about this young man's overreaching. Then I even overheard some talk of putting everything on his credit card!

The second money mistake, according to Ron Blue, is not having a budget. We spend as needs come up rather than according to a plan. If you're sincere about controlling your lifestyle, you must set up a budget. No one likes to talk about budgeting, so maybe a better phrase might be to have a "spending" plan. Ron Blue says, "If you aren't committed to having a budget for at least two years, don't even start." It probably even takes about four years to actually get all your finances in order. Four years of good, solid budgeting before you're stable, and your finances are going in the right direction. Budgets aren't meant to be laws that control us. They are simply meant to be healthy boundaries.

Ron Blue wrote the third-greatest money mistake is on cars. Choosing an expensive car because it reflects "who we are" will be sure to get us in financial trouble. I've heard people say, "I couldn't afford a used car so I bought a new car. I couldn't afford an outlay of cash, but I could afford a small monthly payment." So they end up paying $15,000 because of interest charges instead of $10,000. Strange reasoning! Sadly, many car choices are ego choices.

What's the cheapest car to drive? A used car. Many people I know wouldn't agree with that, especially when we feel like our car is falling apart, and it seems we're spending more on repairs than we would for a new car. The truth, however, is you'd have to spend an awful lot of money on repairs every month to equal the real cost of a new car loan, interest, and higher insurance. Previously owned cars are the way to go. I can testify they have been such a benefit to us personally. Nowadays, with so many buying new, you can get some quality used cars for great prices.

4. Check Out the Facts

> The simple believeth every word: but the prudent
> man looketh well to his going. (Proverbs 14:15)

If we're going to manage well, we need to do our homework. The simple believe every word. *It's got to be true,* we think, *they said so on television, right?* There was research done. Well, who did this so-called research? The simple believes every word, but a prudent person looks out for traps. There are often hidden costs. Banks, for example, make huge amounts of money on fees. They manipulate the timing of deposits and debits and then charge $35.00 for overdraft protection. Banks then call it "free checking"!

Vacation plans are also notorious for hidden costs. By the time you're done with something that was advertised as $799, it is really $2,000! They don't mention that "all inclusive" only meant bread and water!

How was Bernie Madoff able to take some of the smartest people in the world for their money? He was part of a $70 billion dollar fraud. He promised 12 to 14 percent return on every investment, regardless of the market. He would then prove his facts by initially giving steady returns on investments. He took doctors, lawyers, actors, politicians; he bamboozled the brightest and best. The old adage, "If it sounds too good to be true it probably is," is still accurate!

Brothers and sisters, we need discernment! We must know the

Word and live the Word! Check out the facts. One of my friends was getting involved in an aggressive multilevel marketing program. I warned him about it. But he said it was a wonderful product, and everything was on the up and up. After a few months, he came back to me and thanked me for the warning and cautious encouragement. He said he was sitting in the car with two others in the program, and they were bragging about how many people they had "hooked" into this program. They weren't selling product but snagging salesmen! It suddenly dawned on him. He was one of those guys who had been hooked. They weren't selling merchandise but rather people.

5. Have a Plan

> The thoughts of the diligent tend only to plenteousness, but to everyone that is hasty, only to want ... (Proverbs 21:5)

Constructive thinking is not lost time. How can we have a good plan when it comes to money? Let's say you want to buy a car. You ask yourself several questions when it comes to your spending plan. What are you trying to accomplish? How much time do you have to get there? If you want to buy a car, do you need it in a month? A month is different than waiting a year. Your timeline will affect how much you have to save in your spending plan. Those are the first two questions. The third is, where are you now? How much do you have right now? Then finally, what means do you have to reach your goal? If your budget is so tight that you can't afford to save anything, it makes sense that you'd have to generate some sort of additional income.

Scripture says in Proverbs 21:20, "There is a treasure to be desired and oil in the dwelling of the wise." Oil is a staple. It's a treasure. When you find savings, it will be in the dwelling of the wise. Foolish people spend it all. God says oil (or rice or beans, etc.) is to be saved and then distributed as you need it. Don't just consume it, let it out little by little.

People have tried to decide what the best way to track and control spending. There are numerous software programs and apps that can help. Some people do well with them. However, it only tracks spending; it doesn't give any control measures. How can we actually control ourselves?

The best plan is the cash plan. That's what I have done for forty years. The greatest way to get your spending under control is to use cash. I mean cold, hard cash... the money in your pocket. Debit cards are a great way to track your spending, but they don't especially help you *control* your spending as your checking account isn't divided into separate funds. Now, of course, there are some times when using cash doesn't make a whole lot of sense. But with items like groceries, eating out, clothing, personal items, hobbies, and so on, it is very effective.

Get some little envelopes (we have plastic ones in a Daytimer), and put weekly, bi-weekly, or monthly allocations from your income into them. For example, this week I'll put $200 for groceries, $25 for eating out, $ 10 into clothing and $10 for Tennis in the envelopes. When you need to buy a pair of shoes that cost $23 and you don't have $23—you only have $20 in that envelope—you have to take the additional $3 from another envelopes not go on credit.

Another helpful, practical suggestion is dividing your income into sections. Early in my ministry, I read a simple, wonderful book on personal finances. It spoke of a "10-20-70 plan." You subtract your tithe and taxes from your monthly pay, and that's what you have to work with. Divide the balance in three parts: 10 percent for personal savings, 20 percent for debt reduction, and 70 percent to live on. The nice thing about these figures is that if you don't have any debts, you can take that 20 percent allocated for debt reduction and add it to your savings or split it among your giving or living expenses. That 20 percent is what you could also use to save for a car or other item. The remaining 70 percent what you live on. Don't base monthly obligations on gross salary but, rather, on the 70 percent of your after-tithe and after-tax income.

Basically, what is needed is something like the old "cookie jar" savings program our folks used to use. Any extra money they got their hands on went into this restricted fund-that is it was used only for the jar's designated purpose. In like manner, we need to put 10 percent of our gross income into the "tithe jar" and not touch it. Then we place approximately 20 percent into the "government jar" and don't touch it (most of the time, it's put in the jar for us). We then put about 40 percent into the "basic necessities jar." This is for housing, food, and utilities, in order of priority. We almost always have enough income for these amounts so far. Then we place about 10 percent into the "variable necessities jar" for important but not absolutely essential items, such as transportation, clothes, basic insurances, and phone. This does not include a car payment. Then we have the "basic living jar," which includes eating out, recreation, and education. The separate funds act as different "cookie jars" sitting on our counters. We cannot use the cash for anything else but its intended purpose.

About 80 percent of our take-home pay is already obligated, even without any debts to pay. Only after all these separate accounts are funded can we start paying down our debts. Don't take your housing and food income to pay off your debts. That is misusing the money God gave us for higher priorities. Put everything into its proper "cookie jar"-put on the lid, and don't touch it!

6. Thinking Prudently

What is a prudent thinker? It's just having biblical discernment in practical matters. The virtuous woman in Proverbs 31 was a great manager. She considered a field and then she bought it. Can I afford to buy it without taking money from my operating expenses? Is the title to the property good? Is the property really worth what people are saying? Can I actually grow something on this dirt? She thought through all the questions and didn't just buy on impulse; she "considered." Wise people have developed the ability to see something good and proceed. It's important to do our homework.

Let me give you several questions to ask yourself to help keep yourself prudent. Do I really need it? Have I looked at used options (Craigslist, etc.)? Am I planning to use savings for this purchase? Will this purchase result in overrunning any budget category (don't fall into the trap of covering it next month)? Does this decision conform to God's Word (the most important question)? Do I feel a personal conviction about this decision? Is there a caution in your heart?

Do the research, pray about it, and then finally, pull the trigger and go for it.

CHAPTER 6

Financial Wisdom Principle #6
Be Generous

THERE HAS NEVER BEEN a generation of Christians that has been so incredibly blessed materially as the American believer over the last fifty years. At the same time, however, never have there been so many Christians so caught up with possessions as we are. The abundance that is available in the United States is unbelievable. We have machines that do everything. We have gadgets, luxurious cars to drive, huge homes to live in, numerous clothes to wear, and every toy imaginable. We have insurance programs, retirement programs, disability programs, and unemployment programs, you name it. We have done everything possible to insulate ourselves and to make life as comfortable as we possibly can.

You would think that with all the comforts, programs, and incredible possessions we have and the amazing wealth that has been accumulated in America, we would be the most generous generation. But the truth is exactly the opposite! Over these same five decades, charitable giving per capita has unbelievably decreased. In fact a new study by George Barna of *Barna Group* shows that individual tithing-donating 10 % or more of one's income-is practiced by only 5% of American Christians on average. This is really strange to me. What is going on?

Many pastors have told me if they preach on tithing, they face some very disagreeable people. Yet God loves it when His people have a spirit of giving. I read a funny story the other day about a mother who wanted to teach her daughter a moral lesson about giving. So she gave the little girl a quarter and a dollar for church. She told her daughter she could put whatever she wanted in the collection plate and could keep the other for herself. As the two left church, the mother asked her daughter which of the two she gave. The daughter replied, "Well, I was going to give the dollar, but just before the collection plate came to me, the man in the pulpit said we need to be cheerful. And I knew I'd be a lot more cheerful if I gave the quarter ... so that's what I did." One wise guy said God loves a cheerful giver, but my pastor loves any kind of giver! I can vouch for that.

But when we break the cycle of greed, we see what life is really meant to be like. Real living starts where giving starts. A colleague of mine once told me that for him, when his heart gets a little cold or dry, he finds the act of giving sets him on fire. Over the years, I've found the same thing to be true. When I find myself getting down, and things aren't going well in my heart, if I take some twenties and give them to the needs of others ... oh how my heart ignites! There is a scriptural truth behind that. The Bible says in Matthew 6:21, "For where your treasure is, there will your heart be also." When you invest money in the kingdom of God, your heart is in the kingdom of God.

The way of this world and the prevailing mind-set of this world is that we should get as much as we can, regardless of the cost. That's also what most Americans think. Getting rather than giving seems to be the norm, and so many people are in a race for stuff. God's mind-set is far different. His goal is for us to give as much as we can. Our Savoir gave everything. So much, in fact, He became poor. He did so in hope others would become rich. He had all the riches of heaven and glory, yet the Bible states He set that all aside to give salvation to humankind.

There's a story about a man who went to church with his family. On the way home, he complained about everything that had to do with the service that day. The music was too loud, the sermon was too long, the announcements were not understandable, the building was too hot, the people were unfriendly, and on and on. Finally, his son, who had been listening for a while, said, "Dad, you've got to admit this, however. It wasn't a bad show for the dollar you paid!" Ouch.

1. Put God First, and He Will Bless the Rest

Honor the Lord … (Proverbs 3:9)

God wants us to honor Him with everything we have … our clothes, our houses, our cars, and so on. Put God at the top of our spending priorities and give Him the first fruits from our "orchard." Then comes the promise. God promises a "so" or "after that": "so shall your barn filled with plenty." Proverbs 3:10 It doesn't say the barn will be full of Ferraris and other expensive toys. God just says you'll have plenty of the basics.

In chapter 5, I spoke about the 10-20-70 plan. It is a balanced priority system for saving and spending. The first 10 percent after your tithe and taxes to the government, you "tithe" to yourself. That is, you save. Of course, this amount might have to be adjusted if you are a younger family living on one income. The 20 percent goes toward debt reduction. Once that is taken care of (and you purpose to never go into debt again ... amen!), you can put that amount into a savings plan for whatever (house, car, retirement, etc). The final 70 percent is what you live on.

Here's how it works. Simply trust God and give the first tenth of your gross salary or profit somehow or someway. Giving the first tenth, even though we're not under Jewish ceremonial laws today, has always been a pattern of God's people since the earliest days of recorded human history (Genesis 15). Some people I know even have an automatic withdrawal for that 10 percent! That is a great idea for many. There is really no decision to be made about the first tenth—it has always been God's, hands down!

God then puts a blessing on the balance of my resources. He fills our barns. Biblical history records that when the people of Israel were in the wilderness, God kept their shoes and tents from wearing out. From personal experience, I can testify that when I give the tenth, God just stretches the dollar in so many ways that I would never have imagined.

Giving the first fruits and then working with blessed money is such a freeing thing. If I'm robbing God, I'm always going to be second-guessing whether the adversities of life are actually the result of divine discipline. Dr. W.A. Criswell, late pastor of First Baptist Church of Dallas, Texas, told a story about an ambitious businessman who went to his pastor, excited about making something of himself. His Pastor reminded him to always tithe the first 10 percent. The young man promised he would. At that time, he was making about $40 a week. He gave his $4 to the

Lord. It wasn't long until his income increased, and he needed to give $500 to the Lord. It began to really burden him to write that $500 check each week. So he went to the pastor and asked if there was a way he could get out from underneath that covenant he had made. The pastor said he didn't know of any way to be released from that promise. However, he suggested they could pray that God would reduce his income back to $40, so he would have no problem giving $4 every week!

We need to realize there is a supernatural release of funds when we tithe. I read a powerful (true) story. A pastor actually signed and dated this story. It's called, "The Miracle of the Groceries."

In 1984, Mike and his family belonged to my church here on the east coast. On a Sunday evening, the sermon was on sacrificial giving. A special offering was taken at the end of the sermon. The only money in Michael's wallet was a $50 bill. It was supposed to be the money to pay for the family's groceries that week. However, in an act of faith, Mike put the $50 in the offering plate. At the conclusion of the service, Mike and his family went to the parking lot to go home, wondering what they would have for food that week. Within minutes they tearfully and joyfully returned inside the church and asked if I would go outside and see their miracle. Somewhat skeptical, I went outside to their 20-year-old station wagon. Peering through the windows I saw that the interior of their vehicle was completely filled with groceries. Happy for their family, I'd realized that someone had given them a great blessing. Mike told me I was confused and told me that before the service he'd rolled up the windows and locked all the doors and that he had the only key. He further mentioned that when he went back to his car moments ago, the doors were still locked. Mike was convinced that God put those groceries in his car.

It really is supernatural what God will do. For the past four decades, I have personally witnessed when you give to God what's His first, He always blesses the rest!

2. An Increase in Income Comes from Sowing

> There is a way to scatter and to still increase
> and that is withholding more than is meet but it
> tendeth to poverty. (Proverbs 11:24)

It doesn't make human sense that spending is the way to financial security. We usually associate keeping with increase. God, however, says the way to financial security is through spending. The key here is *how* we spend. God promises that if we "scatter," He will make us increase. We're not talking primarily about earthly riches here. We're mainly talking about being rich in our soul. We become the best version of us through giving. There is a little miser living in each of us, and that miser hates to give. We need to starve that little guy. On the other hand, there's someone else living inside of us—the Holy Spirit—that gives us joy. The more we knock down that miser, the more joy can come out.

When we have giving hands, we find they are also getting hands. Greed is a terrible thing. Lee Jenkins calls this "cirrhosis of the giver." He says that is an "acute condition that renders a patient's hands immobile when called on to move in the direction of his or her wallet and then toward the offering plate. This strange malady is clinically unobservable in such surroundings as the golf club, supermarket, clothing store, and restaurant".

Notice where it says, "There is that witholdeth but it tends to poverty." What an interesting thought that is. God says we can actually hurt ourselves by holding on too tightly to our stuff. It tends to poverty. One missionary gave this illustration. He went to a particular indigenous group in Mexico. This particular village had what he described as a "scarcity mentality," that is, a poor person's mentality. A poor person's mentality is, "I can't afford even to give a penny, because I need every penny." Scripturally, a truly rich person's mentality is, "I have been so blessed, I just can't help but bless others." The indigenous group's beliefs affected their whole lives. For example, parents had only one child, because they believed if they had two, their love would have to be split in half. Of course, this meant if you had four children, each child would only receive 25 percent of the parents' love. The scarcity view is that was there's only so much of the "pie." The more people you have, the smaller piece each person gets. As a result of that system, the missionary said it was very hard to reach them with the gospel, because they were very greedy people. He tried to explain God's way to them. He told the people God's way was the abundance mentality: there is 100 percent of everything for everyone who lives. God doesn't cut the pie; He just keeps giving more and more pies … again and again and again. It's incredible when we make that connection in our hearts and minds.

The Bible also says, "More than is meet." It's not wrong to actually withhold some; God is not asking you to give away everything. We should keep some. We should have an organized savings plan. However, some folks just hold onto everything. I know one dear, precious lady who was very plain, and I figured that was just her style. However, after having a conversation with her husband, I came to realize this husband was so tight with money that he wouldn't give his wife any money for makeup!

That's frugality gone crazy. God encourages thriftiness, but being stingy is a whole different ball game. We also need to learn when to pull the trigger, how to let go and live! Sometimes we imagine we are going to run out of money in the future if we give it to God. Think about that. Would the God I honor in my life let me starve because I was foolish in giving too much? Of course not.

It also states in verse 25, "The liberal soul shall be made fat." God isn't promising I'm going to be "rich" but have an inner prosperity that is bursting with spiritual blessing. "And he that waters shall be watered." The most fulfilling life is one full of giving. Nelson Henderson said "The true meaning of life is to plant trees, under whose shade you do not expect to sit"

3. Invest in Those Who Follow

> The good man leaveth an inheritance to his children's children. (Proverbs 13:22)

A wisely distributed inheritance can be a real shot in the arm for children, grandchildren, or others who come after us. Even a few thousand dollars can be such a blessing to them. However, we need to be watchful as we save for the future, so we don't get miserly. Or that we work so hard on saving that we rob people of another inheritance equally important—our time!

We want to leave a financial inheritance, which is a good thing. But the greatest inheritance I can leave is that of a godly example. There are those who have honored the Lord with their resources while they live, and when the end comes, they, like Jesus, have zero dollars in their hands. A godly legacy is the greatest inheritance. If God allows us to leave thousands, praise the Lord! We just give Him all the honor and glory. At the same time, my main goal should not be to leave a pile of money for my children. My first priority should be to strive to give others a godly inheritance. When I do that, I am planting a shade tree for another generation.

One man I know of realized he had an obligation to the future. As he was sitting in church one day, he got to thinking about all the money it takes to run a church. He began to figure out the cost per person to build a new church building. Engineers say it takes forty square feet for each person in a church building. If you multiply that by $200 a square foot to build, it doesn't take long to realize it amounts to a large amount of money: $8,000 per person just for the building! A family of four "costs" $32,000 just to get that building put up. This doesn't include ongoing costs—utility rates, literature costs, landscape fees, salaries, materials. Everything costs lots of money. The man then purposed in his heart that he would tithe over and above his 10 percent to help the next generation.

I like the last part of this verse: "the wealth of the sinner is laid up for the just." There are several ways we can apply this verse, but the sense I'm getting is that if I have not been able to lay up an inheritance like I'd like to, God has money available for my children, sometimes from the people of this world. He has substance available for them. It's as though God is saying, "Don't get too worried about the future, because I have ways to take care of children. I will bless them." The wealth of the sinners is laid up for the just. Every profitable thing that goes on in the world today is ultimately for God's children. Wow! Every bit of information, every new technology or discovery that comes out, is actually for the Christian's benefit. Praise God!

4. Helping a Poor Person Is Actually Helping God.

> He that hath pity on the poor lendeth to the Lord
> and that which he hath will He pay him again.
> (Proverbs 19:17)

All of us should have a heart for the poor. We ought to have a hand for the poor as well. The Bible often refers to sharing your "bread." It doesn't say to share your Rolls Royce (although we should do that, too). It just says to give what you have. Even if it is a small amount, we all should do what we reasonably can. Someone once said that God must love poor people, because He made so many of them. We should all do what we can to help the poor. You may what to do if you've already given all you can. Then I believe we ought to ask for more so we can give more. If we can't give, we ought to pray for their need. Jim Elliot once said, "A man is no fool who gives what he cannot keep to gain which he cannot lose." God promises a guaranteed financial return if you give to the poor.

God wants us to be the kind of people who do what we can to meet people's needs. Proverbs 28:27 says, "He that giveth unto the poor shall not lack but he that hideth his eyes shall have many a curse." Hallelujah! I certainly don't believe that just giving the poor indiscriminate amounts of money is wise. But we ought to look them in the eye—treat them with dignity—and then simply give or not give as we feel is prudent.

5. Wise Gift-Giving Opens Doors

> A gift in secret pacifieth anger and a reward in the
> bosom strong wrath. (Proverbs 21:14)

There's no way to buy a person's love, but there sure is a way to calm people's nerves! Some of you businesspeople can attest to the wisdom of giving something to someone who is disgruntled. It can even be something small, and yet it somehow pacifies the mind.

God gives us the keys for wise giving. It needs to be in secret. We don't ever want to come across as trying to buy people off. The key, I believe, is to look for a true need in our "enemy" and then try to bless him or her secretly. At one point in time, there was someone who had said some very terrible things about the church and me personally. That person eventually needed a recommendation from me. Here was my chance to let that person know exactly what I thought! I mean to tell you, I sat in my chair at my desk and just thought of all the things I could say. But after praying about it, I realized it was best to let God take care of that person's future. I really tried to say any good I knew about that person. I am not sure if my recommendation helped, I hope it did, but I *know* what it did for me—there was a great release! The point is that secret gifts open doors and hearts.

6. Never Hold Back because of Fear

> He coveteth greedily all day long but the righteous
> giveth and spareth not. (Proverbs 21:26)

I love that last part—the righteous do not spare anything. Why do we hold back? It's because we're afraid of running out of something. Aren't you glad God never spares? He just pours and pours out the blessings. God is so lavish. He could have given us one kind of food to eat, but He gave us thousands of types of foods. God just keeps thinking of things for us. He gave so many colors and all sorts of created things. When we're done looking at the things on land, we can go underwater and find a whole other world there! God never stops; He just keeps giving and giving. God is such an amazing giver, and He wants us to be givers, too. Let's not be takers. Let's be givers. In every situation we're in, we ought always to strive to be the giver not the getter.

7. Godly Character Includes Acts of Kindness

> She stretches out her hand to the poor.
> (Proverbs 31:20)

Some folks stretch their hands all right—to get! This wonderful woman, however, stretches out her hand to give to the poor. The concept here is that it actually takes a little bit of work; she has to stretch. There is a real effort put into that. It even says that she "reaches forth" not only to those that are close and in range but to those who are far away from her. She seeks the need and then meets it.

Said in answer to the question: What would you advise a person to do if that person felt a nervous breakdown coming on? Dr. Karl Menniger, well known psychiatrist stated "Leave your house, go across the railroad tracks, find someone who is in need, and do something to help that person."

God gave us energy so we could use it! Let's not be shy about using our efforts and energy for His glory and honor!

CHAPTER 7

Financial Wisdom Principle #7
Stay Free

I BELIEVE THIS CHAPTER'S topic is one of the two most important lessons concerning financial wisdom. Outside of giving, this is the most common money problem. I often tell people if they get rid of debt and stay out of debt and tithe consistently, they won't ever again have another financial problem. Of course, you'll have financial needs and things you'll be praying for. But as far as a "problem," it is the consequences of the choices we have made, so you'll never have another.

Borrowing, paying back, and lending are the least understood of all the financial principles in the Bible, yet it is the number one financial problem. Many modern Christians are surprised to find out the Bible even refers to debt. There are actually many references in the book of Proverbs alone concerning financial freedom that are not that difficult to understand. Still, if you were to ask average Christians in America what the Bible says about debt, they seem to be clueless to the financial wisdom the Bible teaches. Debt is one of Satan's greatest weapons against the peace and stability of a home. We know the Devil's goal is to steal, kill, and destroy (John 10). This applies to our resources as well. Several studies have shown that consumers are likely to spend more money when they pay by credit card. Researchers suggest that "when people pay using credit cards, they do not experience the abstract pain of payment". (The Red and the Black: Mental Accounting of Savings and Debt by Drazen Prelec). It takes each individuals an average of six years to pay off the consumer debt (that's debt other than the house). And that is if they stopped charging today and added nothing to their credit card. Interest charges can cause a terrible situation in a person's life. John Barrymore said "Interest works day and night, in foul weather and fair, to chew at a man's substances with invisible teeth."

Before you whip out that plastic, remember, most adults don't handle those little "bloodsuckers" very well. In fact, nearly 75 percent of Americans who use credit cards make only the minimum payment every month. At that rate, you could spend the next thirty years paying back a $3,000 credit card debt. During that thirty years, you would be giving that financial institution $8,000 free and clear. It is a degrading principle that works against us. Howard Dayton said, "Debt in the U.S. is increasing at a rate of $1,000 per second." He went on to say consumer installment debt had mushroomed to a point where they were taking $1 out of every $4 that consumers earned after taxes just to keep up with the payments! Not even including their home mortgage. It is thought that 50 percent to 60 percent of divorces are based on a financial tension in the home because of debt.

Of all the financial principles the wise man Solomon learned, this is one that is absolutely essential.

1. Beware of Surety

> My son, if thou be surety for thy friend, if thou hast
> stricken thy hand with a stranger ... (Proverbs 6:1)

Let's define "surety." Larry Burkett said that "surety" is a deposit or a pledge given as a security. Actually, the Hebrew word means to intermix, getting entangled with others through unbreakable obligations. According to FreeDictionary.com suretyship is a security against the payment of a debt or a contingent liability. It certainly is a liability or an obligation. Perhaps put more simply, it is a future obligation for something you can't pay for today. Surety is taking on an obligation to pay later without any certain way of paying. That, in essence, is what surety is.

We need to realize the ways of God are different than those of the world. The world's way of doing money works for a time; there are many things the world does that work. But its effectiveness is limited. Someone once wisely said, "The world's ways work for a while but God's ways work all the time." If we knew the future, surety wouldn't be an issue. If we knew, for example, that we would have a job and that we would be able to get so many raises as the years go by, and if we knew we'd never have financial needs or setbacks, of course we'd have a guaranteed way of paying back.

In this verse, it's talking about cosigning an obligation for a friend or a family member. I can tell you this is one of the most financially discouraging situations in the world. When someone you love isn't able to pay just obligations, you will have to pay the loan. One single mom I know provided surety for a loved one for a vehicle. The person wanted a brand-new car but was ultimately unable to make all the payments for some reason. So the single mother now takes care of it.

Why do we become surety for friends or family? Sometimes the reason we cosign is so we won't have to give to the poor. We'll sign a line of credit to release our conscience a little bit, so we don't have to take money out of our account to give to our family or friend! It's often based on a misplaced sense of obligation; we feel compelled because they are family, for example. What I do when a close friend or family member asks to borrow money is to tell them upfront that I don't ever cosign but ask them to give me a day or so to pray and think about if I can do anything. If can help them in some way, I'll try and do that. If not, I just reassure them of my love. But I never cosign.

2. Debt Is a Trap

> Thou art snared with the words of thy mouth.
> Thou art taken with the words of the mouth.
> (Proverbs 6:2)

God emphasizes that our words—whether spoken or written—are things that can get us into deep financial trouble. As we noted earlier, surety is taking on an obligation to pay without certainty of being able to repay. Two major industries are most dependent on surety. The first is the home mortgage industry. The second is the auto industry. Homes and cars are typically our two largest expenditures. Another big concern is a student loan.

As we have seen in America in the mid-2000s, debt eventually catches up to people. Debt has a way of cycling back on you. It is relatively easy to get into debt, and it is one of the hardest things in the world to get out of. Someone once likened debt to an icy slope; it really is. Climbing back up that slope takes time and is very difficult. I have talked to people who are getting a mortgage and say if they can't make their house payments, they will just get out of it somehow. But if we make a promise to pay a certain amount, it seems to me the right thing is to honor that. Many mortgagees, unfortunately, are counting on the shaky ground of state laws of nonrecourse, so the institutions can't sue them for the remaining balance if they short-sell a home. I can tell you God's Word says it would be far better to just not get into that trap in the first place.

Borrowing can get us into a lot of financial trouble. SermonCentral. com says that Larry Burkett, late Christian financial counselor and founder of Crown Ministries, once said that "40 percent of people borrow more than they can make monthly payments on". According to Burkett, the average American family "is only three weeks away from bankruptcy". Why do we have so many financial problems? Is it because we're giving too much money to the kingdom of God? Sadly, no. Ronald J. Sider quotes George Barna in his article *The Scandal of the Evangelical Conscience Why don't Christians live what they preach?* as saying the average American only gives two-fifths of a tithe to the Lord's work.

I could tell you story after story about those who went to a used car lot and bought a used car on credit. The car then gives up the ghost after a couple years into the payment plan, and they are stuck paying for a car that doesn't even run. Debt is a trap.

3. We Should Get out of Debt as Soon as Possible

> Do this, now, my son and deliver thyself when thou art come into the hand of thy friend, go humble thyself and make sure of thy friend. (Proverbs 6:3)

Take some action! You've got to do something and do it now—not a day from now, a week, or a month, but as soon as possible! Notice Solomon's heart: "Do this, now, my son and deliver thyself." He is not angry, he is not upset, he is not condemning. He is loving and delights in his son, like a loving father who wants his son's life to turn out right. Deliver yourself, and do not rely on shaky financial products.

Hallelujah. I am here to promise you God can and will deliver us. "When thou art come into the hand of thy friend." We need to "come" to the people or institutions we have made arrangements with. If they are personal friends, it is even more important to do this. Do not go in with a proud attitude, but humble yourself and "make sure our friend." Few things destroy friendships any quicker or more permanently than debt. The deceitful about thing about debt is that all is quiet for a while. But when the interest starts adding up and a new "pharaoh" comes along, as he did in the book of Exodus chapter 5, how things were structured begins to change. Life can get rough. Now he asks for bricks but gives no straw for the bricks, and things then get very difficult.

Right now, before matters get any worse, use every legitimate means to reduce this debt. "Give not sleep to thine eyes, nor slumber to thine eyelids." (Proverbs 6:4) To delay is to literally play with fire. There is so much financial pressure in debt. I have met many people who are eaten up by that pressure and stress. They try to sleep, drink, or drug their problems away, but it doesn't work. What should we do? Do your homework. Sit down with your creditors and see what you can negotiate to get out of some of the debt. Proverbs 6:5 says to "Deliver thyself as a roe from the hand of the hunter and as a bird from the fowl." Then do everything in your power to stay clear.

Debt resolution is not rocket science. Simply list your debts on a piece of paper. If there are any smaller debts, see if you can negotiate a buyout or otherwise satisfy quickly. After those, the ones with the highest interest rates should be the first ones you go after. Dave Ramsey suggests paying off the smaller debts first, just to get some momentum going. Once you're down to paying one or two larger payments, it seems easier on the mind. Whatever your situation, make a plan and pay those debts. You can do this! It is a lie of the Devil to tell you that you can't.

4. There Is Always a Price to Pay for Debt

> He that is surety for a stranger shall smart for it.
> He that hateth suretiship is sure. (Proverbs 11:15)

The Bible says they "shall" smart. Christians, at times, will acknowledge that debt is mentioned in the Bible but that it's not necessarily a sin. I agree with that concept. But whether it is sin or just unwise, the two are virtually the same to me, except perhaps for a medical emergency. If it's unwise, why would I do it? In this verse, it says we "shall" smart for it. Others say it's not debt if you're borrowing for an appreciating item. Well if the item always appreciated and you built up easily liquidated value, then that would be good, I suppose. For example, nobody thinks the price of homes will go down. But many homes return to thirty-year ago prices, especially in depressed areas. There is no guarantee. That's why the Bible states so simply and so profoundly not to go into debt. It is risky and will come back to bite you.

Let me just say God is not trying to rain on anyone's financial goals parade or kill one's sense of adventure or dreams. God is just trying to provide a safety net for you, a way to stay free.

On this note, let me encourage men to ask their wives for advice concerning ventures. Men can be a little bit more adventuresome or risk oriented, and many women have a great need for security. If a man pays attention, a woman's need for security can be his protection from going too far too fast. It is important to always have a have a solid foundation. I have known several men who took too large of risks with needed savings. It's better to just hang in there over the long haul, try to live, build up some reasonable cash reserves, and then invest with diversity.

5. It Is not Wise to Go into Debt

> A man void of understanding strikes hands and becometh surety in the presence of his friend. (Proverbs 17:18)

Is it sin? Well, it's certainly not wise, which means it's foolish, and that is good enough for me! I say this often, and I stand on this: you will never have another financial problem if you purpose to never go into debt. Let me start by saying up front this issue might be a little sensitive to some Christians. I do not believe the Bible teaches specifically that people "sin" if they involve themselves in surety. I don't especially feel this matter is a "moral law," but, rather, it is a principle. It's similar to the law of gravity. If you break the law of gravity, you will suffer. If you step off a six-foot ledge without a means of taking care of your body, you will suffer, whether it was sin or not! Having said that, I can also state it is possible—and, in fact, probable—that the reason why we go into debt is not right; therefore it is wrong. Violating the law of surety is not especially a moral law unless it is driven by, for example, pride. That would be considered sin.

People sometimes insist they'll never have nice things if they can't go into debt. Perhaps…but so be it. The truth is, however, you can actually have nice things. They may not always be brand-new, but they can still be very nice.

I have been excited to see many Christians I know both get to the place in their business and personal lives where they are doing life by cash, which makes their lives, for the most part, recession-proof. They can slow down or speed up, depending on how God opens doors not on how the economy performs.

6. Be Prudent in Business Lending

> Take his garment that is surety for a stranger …
> (Proverbs 20:16–17)

If a stranger comes to you and wants to borrow money, you pretty much know they have some "big" idea. If they are hungry, of course we should feed them without debt. But it is never about food. Write out the details of the agreement and sign it. A friend once told me "Good understandings make for long friendships." Unfortunately, there are some people who are just in a perpetual financial fix. If they're in pinch now, they'll be in one later. You might say it is unloving to say no. But it is never uncharitable to be prudent.

God calls lending a blessing. It's not even wrong to lend with interest or collateral. Isn't that interesting? We're told in Deuteronomy 15 that if we hear the voice of the Lord, walk with God, and love His law, we will actually be able to lend and not have to be a borrower. I know wonderful Christian people in the real-estate business, banking world, stock market or in development, all industries that depend on debt. God doesn't condemn business lending. In fact, God reminds us that getting reasonable interest from strangers is actually a blessed way to increase our estate! One person said to me, "If you have a savings account, you're just lending to a bank." Well, that's true, but God doesn't condemn lending, He warns about borrowing.

God does, however, prohibit charging interest to a brother (Deuteronomy 23:19). If a brother—or sister—in Christ goes into some business venture and wants to borrow, you should not charge interest. I think, however, it is not wise to get into business him or her at all. There's just a good chance things won't go as planned, and some issues will arise that will cause problems in the church, between families, and among others around them. But if you do deal with strangers, make sure there's ample security and a way to recoup your investment if the stranger doesn't or can't carry through with what has been promised.

7. Watch Out for Unstable Friends

> Be not thou one of them that strike hands.
> (Proverbs 22:26–27)

That's pretty clear. Of course, many of these "friends" are just friends because they want something you have. "If thou hast nothing to pay, why should he take away they bed from under thee?" Proverbs 22:7 It is a sad but true fact that most Americans are in debt because they were born into a debt-dominated society. Lending is not really the problem in credit; it's the borrowing, especially the misuse of borrowing. For most people, the reason they go into debt is so they can get so-called nicer things quicker.

I say this with love, kindness, humbleness, and no condemnation. But for the most part, when people go into debt, it is truly a lack of faith. God says He *will* provide; He *will* provide for needs.

That's either true or false. If He will supply for our needs, we ought to just be patient and wait for the supply to come. At the end of my life, I don't want to say, "Thank God for the Bank of America." I want to say my hope was built on nothing less than Jesus' blood and righteousness! I also want to make sure I don't allow these unstable friends and those who say they'll be able to pay ruin my family's finances.

8. Debt Is a Bondage

> The borrower is a slave to the lender.
> (Proverbs 22:7)

There is no question about this. I can tell you from personal experience that a borrower is a slave. In my early twenties, I got it into my head that my wife should have a big diamond ring. I wanted to be a success, and all the famous and successful preachers I knew had big cars, and their wives had a big diamond ring. So, I thought, *That's what my wife needs*. I found a good jeweler who made custom rings. We didn't have that kind of money, of course, so I put it on a credit card. Oh, what a beautiful ring it was! But this was nothing but pride on my part. Well, that little credit card from the Bank of America ended up making us as a slave for the next four years. Then one day Lynette said that every time she looked at that ring, it bothered her a little. She felt like we'd given over our freedom to the bank. She was a good woman, and we took that ring down to the hockshop and got what we could for it. We used that money toward the debt and then paid it off over the next several months. I never have forgotten that.

So many people have similar stories. Do yourself a favor and google "mortgage stories" or "debt stories" to hear first hand accounts of the many unforeseen troubles that occurred after that person went into debt.

Victor Hugo once said, "A creditor is worse than a slave master, for a master only owns your person, and creditor owns your dignity and at any time can command it." Folks, I tell you again that debt is bondage!

You may have questions about what to do if you're already in debt. I would just say you can only do what you can do. God never expects you to do more than you're able, and getting out of debt takes time. What I can tell you is that I am sure God blesses direction, and if your direction is toward Him and toward right, you can expect victory! If you can sell some things to get out of that debt, you should seriously consider it. If, for example, you're close to the end of your home mortgage or close to the end of your car loan, it probably would be wise to just do what you can to reduce it even faster. But I do know this: if you never decide to be debt free, you never will. It's not going to come automatically. You have to determine that you will be free. I have determined that financial freedom is possible, and for the last twenty-five years, I have lived in financial freedom; to God be the glory! We always had ups and downs and times of need, but God has always supplied.

9. Be Fair in Business Lending

> He that by usury and unjust gain increaseth his
> substance, he shall gather it for him that will pity
> the poor. (Proverbs 28:8)

At first glance, as you read this verse, it may seem that God is actually condemning lending. But what God is saying here is that if you do business lending, you should be fair and loving, and just and kind as much as you possibly can. That doesn't mean you can't insist on the debtor being responsible for what he or she promised. God is simply pointing out that if you lack love and are unkind, God says He will separate us from our substance.

Should Christians ever borrow? Well, no, I don't believe a Christian should borrow. But this doesn't mean you can't make sales contracts with agreed-upon ways for cancellation if the need arises. Can I buy a car or home on a sales contact? Yes, I think you can, but there are definitely some things you need to know about the agreement. The lender and the borrower need to agree beforehand to accept the pledged collateral as the total payment of the outstanding debt. So then at any time along the way, if the seller is willing to accept the property or vehicle back, it can be done. If you can walk away honorably, without any recourse, it is the right contract. When it comes to a house, it would most likely be that you'd have to go through private financing. A lease-to-own option could be one route, as long as there is an early termination clause and no accruing interest on the unpaid balance.

I encourage you in this matter of financial freedom. You can do it. I bless you and praise you in the name of the Lord. I know you can be free! It's my prayer that as you gain this knowledge, you will say, "Yes, Lord, I purpose to break this debt cycle."

CHAPTER 8

Financial Wisdom Principle #8
Keep Your Integrity

Is it possible to be honest in today's business world? Is it possible to take the high road and still get ahead as a Christian? Can we consistently do what's right and still prosper?

Did you know God has placed us as spiritual people in a physical and tangible world? Though we are heavenly minded people, God expects us to live an earthly existence. He could have dropped money down from heaven every day so that we could stay isolated and completely away from the world. But God placed us like little lights, right square in the middle of a materialistic, lying, cheating world! If you truly try to live the biblical way, you will come up against some real issues. Yet God clearly asks us to be the salt and light of our community.

In this series on financial wisdom, we have looked at Bible specifics on finances from just one book—Proverbs. One of the principles we see is that God expects His children to maintain financial integrity. I once saw a cartoon where there was a jail cell full of inmates with two clean-shaven but somewhat disheveled businessmen wearing ties and suits. As they're sitting there among the inmates, one says to the other, "All along, I thought our level of corruption fell well within the community's standards." That really is the issue, isn't it? Standards of right and wrong seem to go up and down with the culture we live in.

Over the last few years, we have seen an assault on integrity as never before. From the White House to the church house, from local sports to the everyday businesspeople, dishonesty is becoming one of the key issues in the financial world. Will Rogers of yesteryear humorously said, "We should live so that we wouldn't be ashamed to sell the family parrot to the town gossip." God's people should live in such a way that we have nothing to hide. Our lives should be open books. Our private and public lives should be the same; there shouldn't be any discrepancies.

1. A Person of Integrity Values People

> The tongue of the just is as choice silver; the heart of the wicked is of little worth. The lips of the righteous feed many. (Proverbs 10:20, 21)

We're talking about "choice silver" and of "having worth." These are financial verses. Each year in America, well-known magazines list the richest people in the world. But perhaps the title should read, "What Are They Worth?" What a person is worth is different in the world's eyes and in God's eyes. In Scripture, God teaches us how to value men and women, and it's certainly not by our money but, rather, according to our wisdom level.

It is possible we may not be very well-to-do in this world's resources but have a mouth that speaks riches of wisdom and has a good understanding of Bible doctrine—and can apply it. A person like that with no agenda, simply doing right with nothing to gain, nothing to lose, and who will simply tell you the truth lovingly is as choice silver! It is a blessing and so refreshing to be around someone who speaks the truth. When chief executives of large companies were asked in a survey what the number-one characteristic needed to be a successful leader was, it was the ability to work with people. The only way you can work with people is when they trust you. Gaining their trust is achieved by being a person of integrity.

2. Watch Where Your Security Lies

> He that trusteth in his riches shall fall but the righteous shall flourish as a branch. (Proverbs 11:2)

There is such a tendency in our lives to lean on *things* rather than the Lord. For example, we tend to lean on our insurance programs, the government, or our possessions rather than leaning and putting our security in the Lord.

Ever had a bum knee? Just when you need it, it gives out on you, and you fall! Have you ever had a cracked tooth? Everything seems okay until you bite down on a big ole juicy steak and then all of a sudden, that thing will just crack apart on you! I admit I have sure had my share of financial "crack-ups"! We are to be careful what and where we sow. When we sow righteousness, we flourish as a branch, because we've sowed in the right place.

Righteous living is like a plant that will continue to grow and produce good fruit.

3. There Is Always a Payday, Someday

> Behold, the righteous shall be recompensed in the earth: much more the wicked and the sinner. (Proverbs 11:31)

We're talking about compensation here. Where and how do we get compensation? "In the earth"; "Much more the wicked and the sinner." In the Scripture, when it says "behold," it's like God is saying, "You can take this one to the bank!" God states there is a payday. Many times our failures and choices, even sins, seemingly go unpunished on this earth. We should know, however, that all sins eventually have to be paid for one way or the other. God reminds us it's just a matter of time.

The good news is that we can turn things around; "the righteous shall be recompensed." Maybe in this life, but for sure in the next! I read a story recently that graphically illustrates how this lack of integrity, this lack of doing right, will prove to be our downfall. Hundreds of years ago in China, the kings and the emperors decided to build a great wall that would protect them from the invasions of surrounding countries. The Great Wall of China is still one of the world's most amazing feats of engineering. People could not climb over it or get through it. But there were gates in the Great Wall of China that enemies were able to go through by bribing the gatekeeper. We get so busy building walls in our life, we forget to teach integrity, which ends up being the very thing that brings us down.

Proverbs 12:14 says, "The recompense of a man's hands shall be rendered unto him." There are big dividends even in this world, if we will do things the right way. According to Proverbs 21:6, "The getting of treasures by a lying tongue is a vanity tossed to and fro of them that seek death." Getting treasures through lying or dishonest labor don't seem to last too long. Have you ever read about people who have won the lottery? The money they received often destroys their lives. And within a few years, the money is gone.

4. Stay Teachable

> Poverty and shame shall be to him that refuseth instruction. (Proverbs 13:18)

Refusing instruction is to our disadvantage. Here are a few self-test questions that might reveal how teachable we are. Can you avoid getting agitated when you disagree with someone? Do you allow someone to speak and to finish without interrupting the person? Can you sit and listen to the truth without being irritated?

A spirit of anarchy has pervaded our country. That spirit of rebellion—and it truly is a spirit—eventually cuts our own throat and leads to poverty.

A few years ago, I talked with a woman who was an acquaintance of our church. I spoke to her about issues and concerns in her finances, which she was bemoaning. I asked if she had a job, and she told me she had had lots of jobs. Come to find out, she had over ten jobs in two years! That's almost a job every two months. Some people have a hard time finding one! She was good at *finding* jobs but not at *keeping* them. After listening to her a bit, I was able to pick up on the fact that she simply did not accept direction very well. If we do not receive instruction, we will not be able to keep a good position. That lack of flexibility and yielding our wills to the will of our employer will eventually bring us down financially.

5, Be Kind to All People

> He that oppresseth the poor, reproacheth his maker. He that honoreth him hath mercy on the poor. (Proverbs 14:31)

We are told that God makes the poor. It is true that sometimes a person is poor, because he or she was disobedient. But I know from experience there are people who don't have as much as others, because they've actually been obedient. Job was obedient, and the Devil took away his resources. Christ didn't even have a place to lay His head. I can think of a precious family in our church who, when they began to grow in the Lord and in their sanctification, realized it would be the wise and best thing for them that the mother stay home and devote her time to her family. Of course, that meant less income. They did right, yet ended up losing money.

Our compassionate God says poor people are to be loved, and He doesn't take kindly to those who take advantage of the poor. I recall George Bush Sr. talking about his years as vice president under Ronald Reagan. He stated that of all the politicians and people of influence he'd met and spoken to, Mr. Reagan was the most down to earth. He was the same to every person, whether it was the man running the elevator or a dignitary of some world power. He was kind to everyone. What a great example!

6. Be Just to Everyone

> A just weight and balance are the Lord's, all the weights of the bag are His work. (Proverbs 16:11)

This "bag," or my lot in life, should be carried out with justice. God is concerned that we be honest in everything, even the small things. God says that in whatever era we live, we should behave with justice. Scales exist for the protection of the seller and the buyer. God teaches us that when a buyer and a seller are negotiating, it should be a win-win situation.

The measure of a person, it is well said, is what he or she will do if never found out—a just weight. Your best security against the future is by doing right today. Proverbs 6:12 reads, "The throne is established by righteousness." If God has blessed you, He has given you a throne, and that's a wonderful place to be. We should always be fair and just, as this will be your best security against future adversity. God establishes righteousness thrones. Do the right thing today, and tomorrow will take care of itself. John D. Rockefeller, one of the richest men of his era, used to say, "Every right implies a responsibility, every opportunity and obligation and every possession, a duty." Yes, let's not take our throne and demand our privileges. Let's continue to work at our duties, and let the future take care of itself. Too many demand their rights. God expects us to assume our responsibilities and stay busy.

7. Choose the Applause of Heaven

> Better it is to be of a humble spirit with the lowly, than to divide the spoil with the proud. (Proverbs 16:19)

God says if we have been blessed with extra others may not have, we must not get proud. It is better to be with the poor but honest people than to hang out with those who are rich with ill- gotten gain. Over the years, it has been proven over and over again that a humble life is the best life. Teamwork always beats the prima donnas. God reminds us the applause of heaven is better than the accolades of humanity.

> A good name is rather to be chosen than great riches and loving favor rather than silver and gold. (Proverbs 22:1)

This is one of my favorite verses. What two things are better than money? A good name and being loved. If you have to sell your name, give up your integrity, or have to lose the loving favor of God, it is too high a price. Many people have looked back only to see they have lost their marriages and families because of dishonest finances. Oh God, keep us from choosing the dollar over our family and caring for our children!

8. Have a Passion to Do Right

> The desire of a man is his kindness. (Proverbs 19:22)

Where our passion is, is where our love and kindness will go. I've heard it said that if you want money, it's yours! I've listened to those on talk radio who say, "If you want riches, you can have them!" Honestly, when it comes to money, there's really no guarantee. You can work for a lifetime and pursue financial success, and in one big sickness, it's all gone! God says it would be better to put your focus on God and others and have a passion for compassion. We used to sing the little song "J.O.Y.—Jesus, Others, You." That's the right order. Jesus ought to be first, others second, and yourself last. Have a passion to bless God and His kingdom.

9. Choose to Live for God's Glory

> Divers weights, and divers measures, both of them are alike abomination to the Lord. (Proverbs 20:10)

God cares about the small things—weights and measures. As Christians, we should try to be as honest, real, and forthright as possible. We are being watched. People often judge God based on how we Christians treat them in business matters. I believe we ought to do our business by the Book (Bible). I believe we ought to do our marriage by the Book. I believe we ought to do our family by the Book. And if we do our checkbook by the Book of books, you can count on God's glory resting on our finances!

What a sad thing it would be to be morally clean yet lose out because of bad business dealings. I remember going to one of our county offices to talk about some building needs we had as a church. I informed him I was the pastor of the church. He said, "Oh yeah, I see you driving all over in your little blue bug." I thought, *"Oh my, that little blue bug is seen by everybody. I'd better be careful. Wherever I go, they are watching!"*

10. Lying, in Reality Is no more than Stealing

> The robbery of the wicked shall destroy them because they refuse to do judgment. (Proverbs 21:7)

Verse 6 sets up this verse by saying if you get money by lying, it is just plain stealing. You might as well have put your hand in someone's pocket and taken the money right out of it! Don't lie to get it over on somebody. Just tell the truth.

Obviously, you can't say everything you know; you still have to be a salesperson. But we should be open and upfront about anything that is a potential issue. I remember reading the little poem titled "Judas." It's a powerful bit of words that reminds us how our personal integrity is of highest value. It goes like this, "Still, as of old, men by themselves are priced.

For thirty pieces of gold, Judas sold himself, not Christ." That's powerful!

11. Walk with God

> By humility and the fear of the Lord are riches, honor, and life. (Proverbs 22:4)

What an unlikely means of having a comfortable lifestyle. No one has ever gone to a financial success seminar and have someone stand up and say, "If you want to be financially successful, you must humble yourself and fear God." That just isn't going to be on the radar. Everybody wants success, and they want it thirty days!

God says, however, not to worry about when you'll retire or living a comfortable lifestyle. Just walk with God. Get up every day and have private time with God. Spend time with Him, pray to God, read the blessed Word, get into church on the Lord's day, pray, and watch Him do mighty things for and through you!

Proverbs 28:6 says, "Better is the poor that walketh in his uprightness than he that is perverse in his ways, through he be rich." For the believer, being poor is only temporary. It is better to pick the less-money route and retain your integrity. Let's leave our success in the hands of God.

> He that by usury and unjust gain increases his substance … (Proverbs 28:8)

God says you can increase your substance by exorbitant interest for a while, but eventually, the providential workings of God that sometimes grind ever so slowly will eventually come back on you. God promises to give our gains to somebody else. I guess there's no better illustration to me than America's housing market burst in 2007. Everybody seems to be pointing the finger of blame at somebody else! The lenders point fingers to the borrowers and the federal government. The borrowers and the federal government point fingers at the lenders and the developers. City governments point fingers at everybody! All people need to realize that if we're trying to get rich by violating the principles of God, it will eventually come back on us. We cannot simply turn our backs to clearly defined scriptural words and imagine we're going to get ahead. Providence does punish, especially if we've taken advantage of others and not done what is right.

12. Lead with Mercy

> The king that faithfully judges the poor, his throne
> shall be established forever. (Proverbs 29:14)

I know those who have resources imagine themselves continuing forever and that nothing will bring them down. But it is uncanny how quickly they can see their estates melt away. God says here that if we want to be established and have financial security for our "throne," we should have a merciful heart. Simply put, look through somebody else's eyes. If we were in the other's situation, what would we like? If we will truly love them and have mercy and lead them with caring, I believe God will establish us.

CHAPTER 9

Financial Wisdom Principle #9
Work Hard

MY HEART AS A pastor, father, grandfather, and a Christian man hurts when I see people struggle. Stress is no fun. But there is a difference between good and bad stress. Paul told Timothy to "Fight the good fight"(1 Timothy 6:12). I don't like fighting—it's not easy—but a good fight is worth it. Getting your finances in order is a good fight. It will take some patience and the grace of God, but you will be grateful you did. Everyone has different concepts on how to be financially successful. However, I have discovered it is best to cooperate with the highest principles I can. It is possible to defy gravity, but it is not likely without help. It's better to cooperate with the laws of God, and you'll find yourself in a better place.

I wish I could be a life coach. I especially wish I could share these words with young couples and young adults. So many of them get into debt at eighteen to twenty years old and are never out of debt again their entire life! They start out and soon get "behind the eight ball," with the erroneous thought it's the best way to get ahead. I'm confident God wants His people to be financially free. I love for God's people to have financial peace. It is such a blessing.

I'm sure this is the same feeling Solomon had for his son. Solomon wrote the book of Proverbs as an older man. These concepts are as though from a father to a son. He is never intolerant about what he says. Always in a loving way, Solomon urges his son to be cautious in his financial matters. God cares about His children's finances, and I'm confident He wants us to have a great life.

Work is a big part of our life. Our lives are filled with jobs and careers. It is through work that God has designed a way to meet our daily needs. It is through work that we find fulfillment and a sense of accomplishment. Being productive is a basic need of all humans. Work also provides an opportunity for Christians to be a light for God.

When I was a young man, I thought work was just a place for evangelism, and it is. Really though, the work itself is a way to glorify God. By doing it well, we are able to shine forth the light of God. Sadly, some people worship their work and become workaholics. Others consider it a necessary evil and drudge through the workday without any joy. One thing I'm sure about is that nothing in the Christian life is without meaning; it's all sacred. In the Old Testament, God filled Bezaleel with His power so that he could do all sorts of work with his hands. He was actually filled with the Holy Spirit to work! In whatever we do, our mission is to be the light of God. The following are some principles about work I know will help you.

1. Think Ahead

> Go to the ant, thou sluggard; consider her ways, and be wise: Which having no guide, overseer, or ruler, Provideth her meat in the summer. (Proverbs6:6–8)

These verses show us how depraved we as humans really are. At times, animals have more sense than we do! God says some of us need to go to animals and see how to live wisely. It states that ants provide, making preparations for the winter in the summer. You can't eat all the harvest at one time. God has made the harvest more than you can eat at one time. We should lay up some for the winter season, when there is no harvest. God never wants us to worry about the future but does want us to have reasonable foresight.

For example, some folks have a different idea about how much money you should have for retirement. You don't want to run out of money, but that's looking at things totally backward. Of course, we are to make prudent preparation. But we should always know God will certainly take care of His children. It is a real temptation to hunker down and brace for the coming storms by pulling back on giving. But that is the last thing we should do. God is the source of our income. We must keep our sources happy! Our main concern should be if we have enough to give not to spend. That's really what God's vision is.

2. Work through the Inconveniences

> Provideth her meat in the summer. (Proverbs 6:8)

If it were easy, it wouldn't be called "work." The ants provide meat in the summer when it's hot. If we learn to work even when it is hard, we will have plenty of prospects for employment. One man I know was a diesel mechanic in Wyoming and would go out in the dead of winter to help start diesel trucks that had frozen up over night. They would go under those rigs with their blowtorch to warm up the frozen fuel and turn it back into a liquid. He said they received anywhere from between $500 to $700 per truck. Sometimes, they helped seventy or eighty trucks a day! They made their meat in the winter.

My daughter, Elizabeth, is a registered nurse and makes a nice rate of pay per hour. She says, however, that nursing is as not easy as you may think. There is some pretty yucky stuff she has to deal with. There's hot and cold in every job. But, you labor and work through it. God wants us to work hard, and if we work hard, we'll make it.

SermonCentral.com records the true story of Joni Eareckson Tada. Joni is a beautiful, Christian woman who was paralyzed from the neck down in an accident. She has gone on to be an inspirational Christian singer, writer, and speaker. During a break at a women's conference she was speaking at, a woman looked at her and said, "Joni, you always look so happy in your wheelchair. I just wish I had your joy. How do you do it?" Joni said, "Can I be honest with you? Just brutally honest?" The woman, of course, agreed. Joni continued,

> I don't do it. Let me just tell you what an average day is like for me ... after my husband, Ken, leaves at 6 a.m., I am alone until 7 a.m. At that point, a friend arrives to get me up. I listen to her make coffee, and I begin to pray for strength and grace because in a few minutes, she's going to get me up and brush my hair and teeth then send me out the

door. A lot of times I just don't have the strength to face the routine another time, I don't have a smile on my face, and I just don't feel good but I know I need God's smile and God's joy. Then my friend comes through the door and I give her a smile that comes directly from Him, it's God's smile that I give to my friend. Really, it's a joy that is hard won.

That's a great statement. People are not born with joy. God-given joy has to be won every day, and it can be won even in the hard times.

3. Be a Self-Starter

Which having no guide, overseer, or ruler. (Proverbs 6:7)

Isn't it a wonderful day when our children get past that parent-directed stage and learn how to self-govern? We have had the privilege of having adult children, before marriage, living at home. They have become self-starters and often surpass us as parents in many areas. They become such a joy to be around! The key to being a self-starter is to have extraordinary purpose. When you have something in the morning to look forward to, you will be a self-starter. It's so vital to find something every day to give you a sense of "I've got to go to work."

Hunger does that, too! When you are hungry and know if you don't work you're not going to have any food, there is amazing motivation. Getting married is also an extraordinary purpose. I've seen some young men who, at seventeen years old, were just sort of everywhere. But before they can marry a girl, they have got to have a good job. Soon after that, they get serious and motivated.

Serving Christ is an extraordinary purpose. When we were doing the initial site work on our first building, it became apparent I would be the project manager and a manual laborer at the same time. There were times I'd be working with only one other person. Some days were hot, and some were very cold. Yet in spite of that, I knew it was a season God truly called me to! There were times that my body, brain, and bones all ached at the same time, all while I pastored a church. How did I keep going? Many times in my heart I would say to myself, *I am serving brother so-and-so. Someday, they are going to walk into this building and be so happy. Someday, their daughter or son is going to get married in this auditorium. Someday, I am going to be able to watch everyone sitting under the patio, having a great time in the Lord.*

I think the same is true for a mother or father. Parents work so hard for so long, but it is for their children … it's for a larger purpose.

4. God Wants Us to Quit Our Bellyaching

> How long wilt thou sleep, O sluggard? when wilt thou arise out of thy sleep? Yet a little sleep, a little slumber, a little folding of the hands to sleep: (Proverbs 6:9–10)

We just want a *little* more sleep. How ridiculous that statement is! Of course no one likes getting up, especially when it is time to work. But if we don't get up, we are going to find ourselves in a hard situation. Someone told me about a skit he saw on the TV. It was called "The Whiner Family." Wendy and Woody Whiner were always whining; they had a nasal pitch to everything they said. They both had diverticulitis, and the only thing they could eat was macaroni and cheese. Then there was Debbie Downer. She would walk in and start grumbling about all the crazy stuff going on in her life. I had to laugh, because we all know somebody who is part of the Whiner family! You may be at work, see someone coming, and think, *I don't know if I can take anymore whining!*

Proverbs 20:4 says, "The sluggard will not plow." Why? It's an excuse about some disease they're going to catch or some bad thing that will happen if they work. Who likes hard work? Who likes to sit out in the freezing cold? Regardless, you still have to plow before you can have a harvest. It's interesting, because plowing is not typically done during the coldest part of the year. Obviously, you don't plow when it is snowing. But when you can plow but come up with some lame excuse not to plow, the consequence Solomon says is that you will be begging in the harvest.

I like the story of Mark Twain. He was given to being a little too "relaxed." He noticed that when he sat under the tree and relaxed, people called him lazy. Of course, he'd be spinning yarns in his head and thinking of stories. To fend off criticism, he started taking a fishing pole with him. He said, "After I brought my fishing pole, people didn't tell me I was lazy anymore … But I found out that when the fish would get on my hook, it was messy and I just didn't like the work. So, I just learned to put a bobber with no hook out there in the water and everyone left me alone!" Lazy people will always find a way to satisfy their desires.

5. Pick a Good, Honest Job

> He that tilleth his land shall be satisfied with bread. (Proverbs 12:11)

It doesn't say you're guaranteed to have steak or a vacation home in the Bahamas. It says that even if the only job you have is plowing, keep at it. If you're plowing behind an ox, your mind is going to start thinking, *I need to do something else!* It always tickles me when people who can't keep a regular job are somehow convinced God has called them into the ministry! They are Christians, but they don't want to work hard. So they decide they want to go into full-time Lord's work. Trust me. You don't want to go into the ministry if you cannot work hard!

"Much food is in the tillage of the poor:" (Proverbs 13:23).What else in life do I really need besides food. If I've a roof over my head and enough food, everything else is fluff. If any additional good happens, praise God! Most of us feel poor, because we don't have all the "stuff" others have. I remember once hearing an actor say, "I wish everybody could have fame and fortune so that they could learn it is not all it appears." When we learn to just be grateful for a full refrigerator, we are most blessed.

Another trick of the Devil to get people to circumvent hard work is through "marketing." I always hold onto my wallet when I meet somebody and find out his or her second job is simply "marketing". I know what that most likely means—they are probably involved in an aggressive multilevel group, and I look like a big piece of fresh meat to them. It's a sad thing when someone tries to prospect a church or make merchandise out of friends. Let me tell you the story of William Colgate. In the early 1900s, at sixteen, William Colgate left his home to work. The only thing he had been taught was how to make soap and candles. He met a Christian canal boat captain, who gave him this advice: "Be a good man, give your heart to Christ, pay to the Lord all that belongs to Him, make honest soap, and I know you will be prosperous." Colgate got to New York and got a position in a soap factory. With the first dollar he earned, he gave a dime. Not long after working there and up the ladder, he actually became part owner and later sole owner of the factory. As the business grew, so did his giving. He gave 20 to 40 percent, and eventually was giving all his income to the Lord. Wow! He said it all started with working hard, paying the Lord His part, and making an honest soap.

6. Be Diligent

> He becometh poor that dealeth with a slack hand but the hand of the diligent maketh rich. (Proverbs 10:4)

God reminds us to stay faithful in the fundamentals of personal finance. There are some basic business techniques that are important no matter what business you're in. God says we need to work hard, which could mean to work hard with your brain as well. Be careful about listening to all these get rich schemes. Just be diligent and work hard.

> Seest a man diligent in his business, he shall stand, before kings. (Proverbs 22::29)

Through diligence, just about any business can become successful, no matter how small or unique. A person I know started the Squeeze Inn. It was a tiny burger joint with only about ten places for people to sit. You would have to "squeeze in" to get in there. But people would line up around the block because of the incredible food. They made a comfortable living on giving people generous portions of good food for a reasonable price.

> Be thou diligent to know the state of thy flocks ... (Proverbs 27:23)

When you are a leader, you have to be concerned about the "three Ds"—dollars, direction, and disciples. You cannot be a business leader unless you're in control of the dollar. You can't be a leader of a business if you're not allowed to plot the direction for your business. You have to be in charge of the disciples—the employees—as well.

7. Don't Waste Opportunities

> He that gathereth in the summer is a wise son: but
> he that sleepeth in the harvest is a son that causeth
> shame. (Proverbs 10:5)

Notice the double responsibility here. There are two things this person is accountable to: he's responsible to the importance of the harvest, of course, but also to his dad. My forefathers have worked hard so that I could have opportunities, so I shouldn't waste them. We owe it to the people who have invested in our lives.

8. Don't Be a Mooch

> The slothful roasteth not that which he took in
> hunting: but the substance of a diligent man is
> precious. (Proverbs 12:27)

There are two ways you can look at this verse. First, it's about one man who makes all the effort to shoot the game, but another man gets to eat it (that is, you are eating something you didn't work for). It is alarming to see the direction America is headed, where takers are above the workers. God warns us about not paying our way.

We imagine being lazy is more relaxing. But the opposite is

actually true, because you are consumed with desire. There is no internal rest, as God made us to work. Did you know that in the garden of Eden (before the fall), humankind was a farmer? Adam was the first farmer. He tended to the crops. We were created to work. It's a healthy thing, and there is a great amount of satisfaction from working hard.

9. Lose the Lip

In all labour there is profit … (Proverbs 14:23)

God says people talk too much. They should just get out there and start working. I remember a real-estate salesman told me some salespeople are always getting ready to get ready. There once was a man who once believed in just "faith." He thought He didn't need to work. He felt as though his prayers alone would lead God to supply all his needs. One day he stood up in church and stated that from that day forward, he was going to trust God to supply and was leaving his job. The first night he prayed very fervently for God to send him food, because he was getting hungry. The next morning he walked outside, expecting food to be right there on his porch. But there was nothing. He figured he hadn't prayed hard enough, so he dedicated the whole next day to praying. There was still no food on his porch. He prayed even more fervently for God to provide nourishment. By now, he was growing incredibly hungry. He cried out, "God, You must provide me with food, or I will die out here!" The next morning he walked out, and there was still no food on his porch. By this time, he was becoming angry with God for not coming through on His promises found in His Word. That afternoon, the man doubled his efforts, rocking back and forth in powerful prayer. Finally, between the words of his prayers, there was a strange silence. In that silence he quietly heard, "I have been answering your prayers; you have just been looking in the wrong direction. Walk outside." He walked outside, looked around, and cried, "God, I don't see any food here on the porch!" He looked up, and above his house was a huge billboard. In black print it read, "Day laborers wanted, lunch provided." God's providing, but He wants us to have a part in it, too!

As much as some may not like to work, the principle is clear—if you don't work, you don't eat. God isn't going to just miraculously drop food down from heaven (like the children of Israel).

> He that laboureth laboureth for himself; for his mouth craveth it of him. (Proverbs 16:26)

Everyone has one problem that is very consistent. Every few hours (and in my case, even quicker), everyone of us are going to get hungry. If we don't get fed, after a little bit, we get grouchy. That is not a flaw. He made us as humans, with needs. Now why would God make us with this need? He made us this way so that we would learn to pray and receive joy when He answers.

He also made us with a hunger factor so that we would learn to work for food. Work is a very healthy and fulfilling thing to do. It builds homes, it builds churches, and it grows families. This desire to eat makes me want to go back to work. If I didn't have a desire to eat, I wouldn't care about work. God has built into us a need to accomplish things. He wants us to be productive. In 2 Thessalonians 3 it says, "If a man will not work, he shouldn't eat." The context of this verse was the local church. Paul was saying there were too many "busybodies" who didn't have any time to work, because they were too busy running around from person to person in the church, gossiping. The best possible remedy for this error is for them not to eat. This can be a great way to motivate a slothful son or daughter as well. If they will not clean their room, they don't get any dinner. Trust me on this ... they will eventually clean their room!

The Bible reminds us that going hungry, at times, is a consequence of slothfulness. Proverbs 19:15 says, "Slothfulness casteth into a deep sleep and an idle soul shall suffer hunger." The slothful person becomes a burden to other people and just sleeps his or her life away. I don't believe the average person realizes just what a blessing working hard is. God has created in us a need to work. It is the right way to fulfill our needs.

10. Plan Your Work, and Work Your Plan

> The thoughts of the diligent tend only to plenteousness but to everyone that is hasty to want. (Proverbs 21:5)

Working hard, however, is only half the battle. Working smart is the other half. We want to make sure we do our "head" work as much as we do our "hand" work. Good, diligent head work is not lost time. Nor is it lazy. A little bit of planning can really help us get more accomplished with our hands. God is saying we ought to work but also work smart. Selling ice cubes in the middle of the winter is obviously not the way to go.

God laid up the wealth of the wicked for the righteous. As Christians, we can tap into that wealth of knowledge and use it to our advantage. Most of us go to unsaved, heathen doctors, for example. It is not God's plan for Christians to avoid unbelievers altogether. We are *in* the world; just don't be *of* the world.

There is a true story about a man who lived in Bihar, India. To access the nearby fields for food and water, he and his fellow villagers had to make a four-mile trek around the mountain. He was fed up with the mountain that was in the way of productive farming. He realized if they could tunnel through the mountain, it would save them hours of travel. So with a hammer and a chisel, he cut a thirty-three feet long, thirteen feet wide tunnel through a solid rock mountain. It took him fourteen years to complete the task. That was hard and smart work.

When I was growing up, my mom read me stories of physicians and scientists. She really wanted me to be a physician, and now I am a doctor … but of souls! One of the biographies she read to me was of the famous scientist Louis Pasteur. We don't realize how many things he blessed our lives with, including pasteurization of milk. He was an incredible scientist. Here's what he said about work: "The secret for my life lies totally in one thing: tenacity." He just never quit. I really believe if we plan our work and are diligent, God will bless us.

11. Put Need over Convenience

> Prepare thy work without, make it fit for thyself
> in the field: and afterwards build thine house.
> (Proverbs 24:27)

Put the urgent before the necessary. A house is a necessary convenience. Of course, we know a house is more than just a convenience. God is saying as important as a house is, you may have to make a priority choice at times. Before you build a beautiful house, you had better make sure you have sufficient income. Build your business so you have a steady income and then turn your attention to your house. Obviously, there is a balance here, because you can't have your family live in a car while you build your business or income.

Here's one way I would apply this. I have noticed too many

people don't "have enough." They just don't ever have enough money to pay their bills. Let's turn the clock back a little bit. God gives us enough for food and shelter. But what happens is that we create obligations for unnecessary things. Yes, a vehicle is necessary but maybe not a *new* car payment. The point I am trying to make is to not obligate your "necessity" money toward things you don't have to. Be very realistic about basic *needs* before you make any commitment to *wants*. My heart goes out to many people, especially young couples, who don't think through their real needs.

12. Wake Up, and Get Up

Love not sleep … (Proverbs 20:13)

I remember being nineteen years old and newly married. I was becoming an assistant pastor at a church, and for some reason, I had a horrible time getting out of bed in the morning. It got so bad that I talked to a visiting fellow pastor about it. He suggested, "Turn your television off at night, and go to bed earlier. When the alarm goes off, drag your carcass out of bed!"

It wasn't very long before I had started a window cleaning business and gotten a commercial account about forty miles from where I lived. This particular job was a restaurant that wanted the windows cleaned by 4 a.m. That surely broke the staying in bed habit!

The Bible says, "Love not sleep …" I do not like that verse. We have to sleep, and it is not even wrong to *enjoy* sleep, just like it is not wrong to enjoy food. After all, God designed our bodies to require rest and with taste buds to consume delicious foods. It's not that it is wrong to love a great night's rest, but we ought to wish we didn't have to! We ought to have such purpose in life that we wish we did not have to sleep a wink, so we could get more done for God! Charles Spurgeon once said, "I have learned over the years that industrious sleep is better than drowsy study." As a pastor who is always studying, I appreciate that quote. Stay alert!

> I went by the field of the slothful, and by the vineyard of the man void of understanding; And, lo, it was all grown over with thorns, and nettles had covered the face thereof. (Proverbs 24:30, 31)

Solomon wasn't poking fun at or looking down on anyone. Yet, he couldn't help but notice some people kept their fields very clean, and others were overgrown with weeds. We see that if humankind was not involved in this world, it would be a terrible place to live. Think about it—weeds, jungles, snakes, critters, and bugs! All you have to do is let a house go for six months and see what happens. God uses humankind to tame this earth. These "earth day" lovers want us to just "let it be." If we'd ever let it be, this world would be very ugly! Now let's apply this spiritually. If I let my children do whatever they want, they would be absolute messes. God has made me a farmer of their minds and a builder of their spirits. I can't just let them go! That'd be like letting the earth go/ God has placed us here for a purpose.

"Then I saw and considered it well" (Proverbs 24:32). We can learn a lot from failures. I'd rather learn from someone else's pain than my own! And verses 33 and 34 read, "Yet a little sleep, a little slumber, a little folding of the hands to sleep: So shall thy poverty come as one that travelleth." We can't help but see the word *little* three times. God is telling us it's the compromises— the shortcuts—that will get us in the end. Working smarter is good. Cutting corners is not. A "little" slumber, a "little" compromise, a "little folding of the hands" will eventually lead us to a large problem. How quickly the resources we thought we had in our hands are stolen from us. Not by someone from the outside but by ourselves. Our own lack of diligence has stolen our own savings.

I'm so glad God in His Word has given us the answers about everything we will face in this life … even our finances. God has given specific, practical principles for every era that always work. The number one question we should ask ourselves concerning financial decisions are if they are wise and biblical. The greatest protection and benefit for our financial well-being is to purpose that we will *always* do what God says. You can do this…you can win financially. You CAN get and stay out of debt. Know that the same God that paid your enormous sin debt through the shed blood of the Lord Jesus Christ can pay off your little credit card bill! My prayer for my sons and daughters, my grandchildren (and those to come!) and all my friends is that you stay free so you can be a champion for God!